# Trespass and protest: policing under the Criminal Justice and Public Order Act 1994

by
Tom Bucke and Zoë James

**A Research, Development and Statistics Directorate Report**

London: Home Office

# Home Office Research Studies

The Home Office Research Studies are reports on research undertaken by or on behalf of the Home Office. They cover the range of subjects for which the Home Secretary has responsibility. Titles in the series are listed at the back of this report (copies are available from the address on the back cover). Other publications produced by the Research, Development and Statistics Directorate include Research Findings, the Research Bulletin, Statistical Bulletins and Statistical Papers.

## The Research, Development and Statistics Directorate

The Research, Development and Statistics Directorate is an integral part of the Home Office, serving the Ministers and the department itself, its services, Parliament and the public through research, development and statistics. Information and knowledge from these sources informs policy development and the management of programmes; their dissemination improves wider public understanding of matters of Home Office concern.

*First published 1998*

*Application for reproduction should be made to the Information and Publications Group, Room 201, Home Office, 50 Queen Anne's Gate, London SW1H 9AT.*

©Crown copyright 1998 ISBN 1 84082 146 9
ISSN 0072 6435

# Foreword

A number of high-profile cases of public disorder during the late 1980s and early 1990s led to provisions in the Criminal Justice and Public Order Act (CJPOA) 1994 dealing with 'collective trespass or nuisance on land'. In particular, powers and offences were created for the police to deal with cases of disorder involving 'New Age Travellers', people attending 'raves' and hunt saboteurs. These provisions attracted a great deal of debate during their passage through Parliament, and were the main focus of a series of large-scale public demonstrations protesting about the CJPOA. This report examines how these provisions have been used by the police to deal with public disorder involving private land, alternative lifestyles and contemporary forms of protest.

The findings indicate variations in the extent to which forces have made use of the provisions, and in the size, seriousness and duration of the related events. The number of cases resulting in prosecution also varied considerably between offences. The extent to which the CJPOA provisions were drawn upon and the ways in which they were used were found to be strongly influenced by existing police practices and especially approaches to public order policing. Overall, one of the biggest consequences of the provisions was to put the police in a much more secure legal position when policing particular types of disorder.

DAVID MOXON
Head of Crime and Criminal Justice Unit
Research, Development and Statistics Directorate

# Acknowledgements

We would like to thank the many police officers in the forces we visited who were kind enough to give up their time to be interviewed. We are especially grateful to those working in the Northern and Southern Intelligence Units, whose efforts made it possible for us to contact police officers with experience of using the CJPOA public order powers. Thanks should also go to Rob Street who assisted us in analysing the vast amount of qualitative data we collected and to David Brown whose advice and support throughout the research was highly valued.

# Contents

# Summary

This research study examines the main public order provisions contained in the Criminal Justice and Public Order Act (CJPOA) 1994. These concern: trespass on land by groups such as 'New Age Travellers' and gypsies; unlicensed parties called 'raves'; and aggravated trespass associated with animal rights and environmental protesters.[1] Under these provisions the police now have the power to: direct people from open land; seize vehicles and sound equipment; and direct people not to proceed towards a particular event. In addition, the CJPOA created a new set of criminal offences relating to specific forms of behaviour by trespassers and to non-compliance with directions given by police officers.

The study examines the use of these provisions by the police. It focuses, firstly, upon the extent to which the provisions have been used and the degree to which their use has resulted in cautions and court proceedings and, secondly, upon the ways in which officers have applied the provisions, the impact of their use and the issues which have emerged. The study draws upon interviews conducted in 14 police forces with a total of 64 officers who have policed the kinds of disorder addressed by the CJPOA provisions, as well as upon police and court statistics. The main findings of the research are as follows.

## Trespass on land

The CJPOA gave the police the power to direct trespassers illegally residing on a piece of land to leave the site. It is an offence to ignore a police direction and to return to a site within three months of having been directed away. When a direction has been ignored the police have the power to seize trespassers' vehicles.

- The CJPOA provisions were found to have been applied to both New Age Travellers and gypsies. However, police willingness to direct gypsies from land using the provisions tended to vary from one force to another. Police time and resources were also an issue, with at least one force limiting its involvement in cases of trespass by not using its CJPOA powers and thereby leaving landowners and local authorities with responsibility in this area.

---

[1]  This report does not examine the CJPOA public order provisions concerning trespassory assemblies, unauthorised vehicular campers and squatters.

- The identification of an illegal encampment usually led to some discussion between the police, local authority and landowner as to the best course of action. Once the police officially became involved, they tended to take several interim steps before resorting to full enforcement of the CJPOA provisions.

- In the experience of those officers interviewed, directions to trespassers to leave a site always led to the site being cleared. However, it was often necessary to back up directions before they became effective. This could involve: a large number of officers having to attend the site, with the associated threat of arrest and seizure of vehicles; the making of token arrests; and the towing of one or two vehicles onto the highway.

- Difficulties recording the identities of trespassers meant that officers rarely had sufficient evidence to prove that someone had returned to a site after being directed away. As a result, if a group of trespassers was thought to have returned to a site within three months officers would simply give another direction to leave, rather than make an arrest.

- Officers were very wary about using their powers to seize vehicles under the CJPOA provisions due to the high level of organisation and expense involved. While not discounting totally the seizure of vehicles, officers generally felt that a situation would have to be very serious to warrant this form of action.

- Officers stated that the use of the provisions could lead to disruptive or sizeable groups of New Age Travellers and gypsies moving to another illegal site and simply displacing any problems.

- Police officers directed trespassers from land 67 times in 1995; the numbers of people and vehicles evicted on each occasion varied greatly. Prosecutions under the provisions were very rare, with a total of eight prosecutions occurring during 1995 and 1996.

## Raves

Under the CJPOA the police have the power to direct people to leave the site of a rave, seize sound equipment and direct people hoping to attend away from the event. It is an offence to ignore a police officer's directions and to return to the site of a rave within seven days of being directed away.

- The way in which the rave provisions were used depended on when the police came to hear that one was to be held. If informed early enough, officers might try to stop the rave by clearing the site and turning back those travelling to the event. If a rave was in progress, officers might 'contain' it by preventing others attending, using police stop checks.

- The wording of the provisions had created some difficulties and, in particular, the meaning of the terms 'making preparations for a rave', 'land' and 'open air'. In at least one force officers had refrained from using the rave measures until these terms had been clarified through judicial decisions.

- The power to arrest someone for returning to a rave, having been directed away, was rarely, if ever, used. Those initially complying with officers' directions rarely had their personal details taken, thereby making an alleged return to a rave hard to prove. If someone was thought to have returned it was likely that they would simply be directed away again.

- The power to seize sound equipment was rarely used since officers tended to persuade those responsible for it to remove it. When sound equipment was being driven to a rave, officers might seek to prevent it reaching the site using other non-CJPOA powers rather than seizing it. Officers were unwilling to enter a rave and seize sound equipment once it had started because of the dangers facing them.

- Under the provisions the police can stop people proceeding to a rave only when those at the site of the rave have been directed to leave by officers. However, some officers were unclear about this and on occasions had turned people away from a rave when no official direction had been given to those at the site of the event.

- Most people tended to comply with directions when they were issued. A high level of compliance meant a low number of court proceedings, with only seven people being prosecuted for failing to leave the site of a rave, and none for ignoring an officer's direction not to proceed towards such an event.

## Aggravated trespass

The CJPOA created the new offence of aggravated trespass; it is committed when a person trespasses on land and seeks to intimidate, obstruct or disrupt a lawful activity. The police also have the power to direct from land people they believe have committed or intend to commit aggravated trespass. It is an offence to ignore such a direction or to return to that place within seven days of being directed away.

## Fox hunting

- The police used three main strategies to police hunts. The 'intelligence-led' and 'pro-active' approaches both made use of the CJPOA measures. The 'agreement-led' approach involved officers, as part of wider negotiations, agreeing not to use the CJPOA measures in return for specific concessions from local saboteurs.

- Officers generally welcomed the CJPOA measures, but emphasised that whether they were used depended on the number of police at the scene and the discretion of individual officers.

- Officers interpreted the following activities as constituting aggravated trespass by saboteurs: the wearing of balaclavas and masks; possession of staves; shouting abuse at members of the hunt; jumping in front of horses; obstructing the digging of a fox from its earth; the use of anti-scent spray; and attempts to 'draw' the hounds.

- Saboteurs and protesters generally complied with officers' directions to leave land. However, dispute about whether the person making the direction was the 'senior officer at the scene' led to a number of prosecutions being dismissed at court.

- It was rare for people to be arrested for returning to land after having been directed from it. This was for similar reasons to those given in relation to trespass on land and raves. Officers were uncertain about whether returning to land meant a return to exactly the same spot, same field or a wider area.

- Providing enough evidence for a successful prosecution was said to be difficult, although the use of video equipment had been found effective. Discontinuance by the CPS and the failure of a number of cases in court had led to frustration among officers, with some complaining that the CJPOA provisions now had little deterrent effect on saboteurs.

## *Environmental protest*

- The police operation in response to protests against the building of the Newbury bypass involved the greatest single use of the CJPOA public order provisions. During the police operation 356 arrests were made for aggravated trespass. Of those arrested, 59 were cautioned and 258 prosecuted.

- The large number of arrests for aggravated trespass at Newbury partly reflects the level of conflict on the site, but also the nature and scale of the police response. Unlike at a fox hunt, the police at Newbury were aware of when disorder was going to occur and where it was likely to happen. Sufficient officers were therefore deployed at the right times and places to deal with disorder and were able to utilise the available provisions.

- The powers to arrest for aggravated trespass were viewed as a positive development by officers, who felt that the use of breach of the peace at previous road protests was inappropriate for the behaviour in question and of limited value in terms of the sanctions involved.

- The power to direct people from land was rarely used at Newbury. This was mainly because other legislation appeared to offer some counter protection to those living on the site and threw the use of this power into question.

- At Newbury, and in other instances of environmental protest, prosecutions for aggravated trespass tended to be challenged at court on the grounds that the work being obstructed or disrupted was unlawful. Challenges might focus on health and safety procedures or on other related regulations.

- Police figures for England and Wales show that a total of 122 people were arrested for aggravated trespass during 1995 and that directions to leave land were given on 17 occasions. Court statistics show that 359 people were prosecuted for aggravated trespass in 1996, compared to 111 in 1995. Just over half of those prosecuted for aggravated trespass were convicted.

## Conclusions

- Half the police forces in England and Wales used the new CJPOA provisions during 1995.

- Formal action by way of a police caution or prosecution was relatively infrequent. This was because the directions, or even the threat of their use, was commonly found to resolve situations without the need for arrests.

- A strong theme emerging from the research was how use of the powers could vary from force to force, division to division and incident to incident. Clearly the pattern of public disorder is not random; however three other factors had a strong influence on these variations. These were:

  - police willingness to use the CJPOA powers, with some forces and divisions enthusiastically and frequently applying the powers while others had formal or informal policies which restricted their application;

  - whether the police had been given prior warning of possible public disorder, and had deployed officers in good time and sufficient numbers for the CJPOA to be utilised;

  - individual officers' skills in managing public order situations and keeping the peace. The *possibility* of the provisions being used could provide a background to public order encounters, but whether and how they were applied depended on the skills and experience of officers.

- In the past the police had dealt with situations covered by the CJPOA using pre-existing powers and offences. These included sections of the Public Order Act 1986, common law breach of the peace, public nuisance and criminal damage. On other occasions, when no law or powers were clearly applicable, officers relied on their general authority. Overall, the introduction of the CJPOA did not appear to have led to a significant change in officers' approach to disorder or an expansion of the types of situation they attended. However, the use of the CJPOA provisions rather pre-existing powers resulted in officers being placed in a *stronger legal position* when dealing with cases of disorder.

# 1 Introduction

The Criminal Justice and Public Order Act (CJPOA) 1994 introduced a series of provisions for the police to deal with 'collective trespass or nuisance on land'. The most high profile of these provisions were designed to address the problems posed by 'New Age Travellers', people attending 'raves' and hunt saboteurs[1]. This study describes these provisions and examines how they have been used by the police during the first 18 months of their existence.

## Background to the research

The creation of the public order provisions focused upon in this study was partly a response to various well-publicised cases of disorder during the late 1980s and early 1990s. These included several large unlicensed rave parties during the summers of 1989 and 1990, and the Castlemorton free festival, held in Worcestershire during May 1992. Proponents of the provisions described them as protecting rural communities that in the past had suffered from mass invasions by trespassers, causing both destruction to property and distress to residents[2]. The provisions were also designed to deal with the actions of people like animal rights protesters who trespassed on land and disrupted the lawful activities of others, such as those involved in fieldsports. The CJPOA's public order provisions were both the subject of much debate during their passage through Parliament and the main focus of a series of large-scale public demonstrations against the Act. The provisions were criticised in particular for:

- extending the criminal law to the area of trespass that in the past had been dealt with mainly under civil law (Liberty, 1995a);

- criminalising the lifestyles of New Age Travellers and young people involved in the 1990s dance scene, and forms of protest associated with animal rights campaigners (Liberty, 1995a);

- being too wide-ranging, and having the potential to be used in unanticipated and inappropriate situations (Thornton, 1994; Lord McIntosh, *Hansard*, Lords, 7 July 1994, col 1489; Penal Affairs Consortium, 1994);

---

1  The CJPOA also introduced public order provisions directed at trespassory assemblies, unauthorised vehicular campers and squatters.

2  A full statement on the kinds of behaviour that the provisions sought to counter was given by the then Home Secretary, Michael Howard, in the House of Commons (*Hansard*, Commons, 11 January 1994, col 29).

- being too draconian since the penalties for those convicted of offences created by the Act could include a custodial sentence (Liberty, 1995a);

- being unnecessary since they covered behaviour allegedly addressed by other criminal offences (Penal Affairs Consortium, 1994; Card and Ward, 1994).

Despite opposition, public order provisions relating to 'trespass on land', 'raves' and 'aggravated trespass' were among those which successfully passed into law. The police acquired powers to direct from open land people engaged in, or about to engage in, certain activities and events. Officers were also given the power, under certain circumstances, to seize the property of people being directed away from a piece of land as well as to direct people not to proceed towards a particular event. In addition, specific actions by trespassers and non-compliance with certain directions given by police officers were made criminal offences. The majority of these powers and offences came into force when the CJPOA received Royal Assent on 3 November 1994.

This study specifically addresses the CJPOA's provisions concerning: trespass on land by groups such as New Age Travellers and gypsies; unlicensed parties called raves; and aggravated trespass associated with animal rights and environmental protesters. The study examines the practical use of these provisions by the police, and in doing so focuses upon the following two areas.

- The extent to which the provisions have been used and the degree to which their use has resulted in cautions and court proceedings.

- The ways in which officers have applied the provisions, the impact of their use and the issues that have emerged[3].

## Methodology

As part of a wider assessment of the working of the CJPOA, the Home Office monitored the use of the new public order provisions during 1995. This was done by police forces reporting any use of the provisions and any related arrests to officers based in the Northern and Southern Intelligence Units[4]. The Home Office also collected statistics on cautions, prosecutions and convictions for the new offences. These two sets of figures provided an indication of the extent to which the provisions had been used by the police and the degree to which formal action was being taken against those concerned.

3.  Further research by Zoë James examines the experiences and perspectives of those groups who have had the CJPOA provisions applied to them by the police.
4  These units are based in the Cumbria and Wiltshire Constabularies and are responsible for collecting details on people known or suspected of committing trespass and related criminal activities.

While the above sets of figures provided some basic data on the extent to which the CJPOA provisions were used they did not provide any insight into *how* they were used or their *impact*. These issues were focused upon in the main part of the research which involved interviews with officers policing the situations addressed by the provisions. These interviews were based on a sample of officers with a background in public order policing and a range of experience in using the CJPOA provisions. The events focused upon in interviews varied widely in terms of the extent of disorder, level of policing and duration of the incident. For example, an illegal rave might require a large number of police for just a few hours, while a fox hunt could involve a small number of officers attending weekend meets throughout a season lasting several months. Interviews with officers examined public order policing prior to the CJPOA and the use of the Act's provisions during the first 18 months that they were available.

A total of 64 police officers from 14 police forces[5], were interviewed, with the majority being inspectors or chief inspectors since these officers were traditionally in charge of the public order events in question. Because interviews drew on their experience of policing a large number of public order situations over many years it is difficult to say exactly how many incidents were covered by the research. However, in relation to incidents occurring after the CJPOA was implemented, the research covered approximately 25 cases of trespass on land, ten illegal raves and, in terms of aggravated trespass, 15 fox hunts and six cases of environmental protest. The interviews were conducted during the first seven months of 1996.

## Structure of the report

Each set of public order provisions is dealt with in a separate chapter. Chapter Two concerns police use of the provisions relating to trespass on land, which were designed to deal with New Age Travellers, and Chapter Three focuses upon those relating to raves. Chapter Four covers two areas of aggravated trespass, namely fox hunting and environmental protest. Each of these chapters begins by outlining the related powers and offences, and then goes on to describe the main findings from interviews with police officers. At the end of each chapter figures are presented on the use of the provisions across England and Wales by the police during 1995, together with official statistics on the number of people cautioned, prosecuted and convicted during 1995 and 1996. Chapter Five draws together the findings and discusses the main issues to emerge.

---

5    The 14 police forces were Avon and Somerset, Cumbria, Essex, Greater Manchester, Hampshire, Kent, Lincolnshire, Nottinghamshire, Surrey, Sussex, Thames Valley, Warwickshire, West Mercia, Wiltshire.

# 2 Trespass on land

## Background to the provisions

The early to mid-1980s saw a number of mass trespasses onto agricultural land by 'Hippies', 'Hells Angels' and other groups, involving damage to property and threats to local inhabitants[1]. As a direct result, s39 of the Public Order Act 1986 was created to give the police the power to direct trespassers from land. The power could be exercised when a senior officer was sure that trespassers had brought 12 or more vehicles to a site on which they were seeking to reside, had caused damage to the land, and had been asked to leave by the landowner. Under s39 it was an offence not to leave the land once directed away by an officer and to return to the land within a three-month period of the direction.

Despite the availability of this power, in the early 1990s a great deal of publicity was given to disturbances by large groups of New Age Travellers encamped in various rural locations affecting local residents and landowners. The most high-profile disturbance occurred during late May 1992 at a New Age Travellers' camp on common land close to the village of Castlemorton, Worcestershire. An estimated 20,000 people attended the camp during its first weekend, in what became a 'free festival' lasting nine days. As well as besieging the 800 people living on or around the common, the event involved serious noise disturbance, a number of burglaries, damage to property, drug dealing, threats and acts of violence, and public-health problems (see Baxter, 1992). The event gained a high degree of media coverage, and while residents' anger was directed mainly at those attending the camp, the West Mercia police were also criticised for not intervening and attempting to clear the site. Two years later, Castlemorton was cited by Earl Ferrers, the government spokesperson in the House of Lords, to highlight the 'destruction and distress which are caused mainly to rural communities by trespassers' and as 'demonstrating only too clearly a serious problem which had to be addressed' (*Hansard*, Lords, 25 April 1994, col 384). As a result, s39 of the Public Order Act 1986 was repealed and replaced by a stronger set of powers contained in the CJPOA.

---

1  One of the better known examples of this concerned the 'Peace Convoy' consisting of 100 vehicles and 300 New Age Travellers which encamped on farmland in Somerset during May 1986 in readiness for the summer solstice festival at Stonehenge.

## The CJPOA provisions

The police now have two powers to deal with trespass on land.

### The power to direct trespassers to leave land

Under s61 of the CJPOA a 'senior officer present at the scene' can direct trespassers to leave land if he/she is reasonably satisfied that two or more trespassers are there with the purpose of residing on the land and that the occupier has taken reasonable steps to ask them to leave. In addition, the officer must be reasonably satisfied that at least one of the following conditions applies.

- One or more of the trespassers has caused damage to the land or property on it.

- One or more of the trespassers has used threatening, abusive or insulting words or behaviour towards the occupier, a family member, or employee or agent.

- They have at least six vehicles on the land.

A senior police officer can direct people to leave even if they have not entered the land as trespassers (e.g. they were initially given permission by the occupier to enter the land); however, one of the above three conditions must apply *after* they have become trespassers.

Once an officer has given someone a direction to leave land an offence is committed if that person fails to leave the land 'as soon as reasonably practicable' or enters the land again as a trespasser within the next three months. Under these circumstances it is a statutory defence if the accused can show either that they were not trespassing, or that they had reasonable excuse for failing to leave as soon as practicable, or for entering the land again (s61(6)). Offences under s61 are summary only (they can only be tried at a magistrates' court). The maximum punishment is three months' imprisonment, or a fine of up to £2,500, or both.

### The power to seize vehicles

When the police have given a direction to leave land but trespassers have failed to leave or have returned, officers have the power under s62 to seize and remove vehicles which the trespassers have on the site. 'Vehicle' includes caravans, motor-campers, buses or coaches adapted for human habitation, and can extend to any bicycle, cart or chassis. A vehicle does not have to be roadworthy, but must be in the control or possession of the trespassers. Officers may therefore seize a vehicle that belongs to the owner of the land but which has been commandeered by trespassers.

Similar powers were extended to local authorities, with s77 of the CJPOA enabling them to direct people residing in vehicles on an unauthorised site to leave that land and remove their vehicles and other property from it. If those resident on the land refuse to move, under s78 a local authority can seek an order from a magistrates' court for their removal.

The provisions concerning trespass on land generated a great deal of public and parliamentary debate. A central part of this debate concerned the legal status of trespass which, apart from s39 of the Public Order Act 1986, had been dealt with traditionally by civil rather than criminal law. The provisions contained in the CJPOA were criticised as criminalising the way of life led by travellers, and as extending the criminal law into new areas that had been dealt with previously by county court eviction procedures.

## Groups affected

The new provisions were created as a result of, and with the intention of preventing, mass trespass by New Age Travellers. However, during the CJPOA's passage through Parliament it was made clearby David Maclean, a government spokesperson, that the provisions could be used against 'others invading land' (*Hansard*, Commons, 13 April 1994, col 296). Previous concern about s39 of the Public Order Act 1986 being used against groups for whom it was not designed led the Association of Chief Police Officers (ACPO) to advise, in a set of *Good Practice Guidelines*, that s39 was not intended for, and so should not be used against, 'genuine' gypsies (quoted in Card and Ward, 1994)[2]. However, interviews with officers indicated that s39 had been used in relation to this group when serious damage to land or property had occurred.

The CJPOA provisions were found to have been applied to both New Age Travellers and gypsies, but that the use of the powers in relation to the latter group varied across forces[3]. In at least two forces visited officers stated that they simply did not use the trespass provisions against gypsies since it was felt that this would be inappropriate. Other forces had used the provisions on numerous occasions to remove gypsies from various sites. However, in at least one force this use of the provisions had been replaced by a new policy that reduced their use to 'extreme cases' involving large disruptive groups and/or large-scale damage to property. Here officers were encouraged to

---

2    For a definition of 'gypsy' see Appendix A.
3    A report on the use of the CJPOA public order provisions by Liberty (1995b) also found variations in the use of s61 across forces and local authorities.

work closely with the local authority, and to create 'Positive Prevention Working Parties' with local authority representatives. Without sufficient authorised sites in the area, these working parties sought to persuade Gypsies to vacate inappropriate encampments in favour of 'temporary tolerated sites'. The policy aimed to reduce police involvement in dealing with illegal camping sites and emphasised that the local authority was seen as holding the prime responsibility for enforcing the removal of illegal campers. However, officers could be used to support the local authority when carrying out evictions in order to prevent possible breaches of the peace. Important developments concerning local authorities[4] and their impact on police use of the trespass on land provisions are discussed below.

## Initial stages in the use of the provisions

In the majority of cases police officers were informed about an illegal encampment through calls from the public or a local authority. Only in cases involving large convoys of New Age Travellers were officers informed via the Northern or Southern Intelligence Units, or a neighbouring police force. The sites in question included car parks, playing fields, farmland, industrial estates, vacant or derelict land, business parks, grass verges and building sites. Threats or abuse directed at the occupier of the land were rarely reported, with police action more likely to be based on damage to the land or property on it. The CJPOA does not stipulate the extent of damage required to merit action or whether it has to be deliberate or accidental. Examples described in the research included: churned up ground caused by heavy vehicles; diesel spillages; animal and human excrement; scorched earth from fires; destroyed fencing; and spoiled crops. The dumping of litter and rubbish on the land was often mentioned and, while illegal under other legislation, does not appear to fall within the legal category of 'damage' (see Card and Ward, 1994). Another problem police officers associated with encampments of trespassers was a rise in property offences in the local area.

The discovery of a New Age Traveller or gypsy site usually led to discussions between the police, the local authority and the owner about who should take responsibility. Formally, the law provides a graduated response to trespassing travellers according to the seriousness of the nuisance. In a simple case of trespass a landowner can apply for an injunction; in other cases the local authority can use its own powers under the CJPOA to clear a site; and in more serious cases the police can use their powers. However, in practice, the division between these courses of action was not always clear.

---

4    The CJPOA removed the duty imposed on local authorities by the Caravan Sites Act 1968 to provide sites for gypsies and repealed the provisions of the Local Government, Planning and Land Act 1980 authorising central government to pay grants to local authorities for capital expenditure on providing gypsy caravan sites.

One factor which could influence police involvement concerned the ownership of the land on which the trespass was taking place. In cases where there was evidence of damage to land or property the police might not always take action. Instead, where the land in question belonged to a public organisation (such as the Forestry Commission), a large private company, or a major landowner the police looked, at least initially, to the owner to use the civil law to remove the trespassers, rather than drawing on public funds. Some landowners clearly hoped the police would become involved and expressed frustration when this did not occur. However, officers were much more likely to act when the site belonged to an individual, or a small organisation without its own legal department.

A local authority might help those not receiving police help with applications for evictions, although this course of action could be expensive for the landowner. Faced with a potentially long and costly procedure to remove the trespassers some landowners looked to common law powers that allowed them to evict trespassers using reasonable force. Officers cited occasions when this course of action had the potential to lead to disorder, such as when landowners had towed vehicles off land or had blocked off exit points from a site and negotiated with the trespassers about their departure from it.

> 'Certainly one of them was done through legal means, taking their own action. Another one involved a bit of pressure. Using JCBs and things like that. Rolling up and sort of waving the JCB shovels at them or something in that nature.' Interviewee 15-39-21

In some cases of trespass, rather than being actively involved the landowner could not be traced by the police or local authority. Establishing swiftly who actually owned a piece of land and locating them could be difficult, particularly when a site was being developed or the owner lived outside the area. If these circumstances were combined with trespassers causing disorder or being a serious nuisance then officers might become involved and look to other powers and courses of action to move the group on.

Police involvement could also depend on the level of disorder associated with the trespassers. This could lead to strained relations between the police and local authority, with debates surrounding who should take responsibility for a particular case of trespass. ACPO guidance to police forces on the use of s61 states that:

> 'The police, as officers of the law, are responsible for public order, and the prevention and detection of crime. It is therefore only in such circumstances that the use of section 61 should be considered as a primary response.' (ACPO, 1996)

In line with this guidance a number of senior officers had taken the position that the behaviour and disturbance caused by a group of trespassers in their area were not serious enough to warrant police involvement. However, some local authorities felt that the police were being too restrictive and argued that level of nuisance associated with particular sites meant that police involvement was exactly what was required. Despite the ACPO guidance some officers had felt compelled to act and had used s61 following substantial complaints from local residents, or when a landowner had tried and failed to remove trespassers from a piece of land. Linked to this issue was a concern among forces about police time and resources being increasingly committed to cases of trespass. As a result, at least one force (not among those included in this research) had adopted a policy of not using s61, thereby leaving landowners and local authorities with responsibility for trespass.

Overall, police willingness to become involved in cases of trespass was found to vary significantly between forces and between individual divisions within a force. As a result, the circumstances likely to trigger police action differ from place to place.

## Giving the direction to leave land (s61)

Once the police had become involved in a case of trespass, a battle of nerves tended to develop between officers and those on the site, based on how far each side thought the other was prepared to go. This could escalate through a number of stages, leading to the full enforcement of the provisions. New Age Travellers were described as being particularly well prepared for this battle, with some having a thorough knowledge of the CJPOA provisions and their rights, access to legal support[5], and, on occasion, the ability to call in the local media to publicise their case.

The first move by officers in several cases was, without recourse to the CJPOA's provisions, simply to tell those people on the site that they must go. If this did not work officers would then serve a s61 direction to leave. This might involve a verbal direction to all those on the site via a loud hailer, but was usually done by officers handing out leaflets outlining the direction and explaining on what ground it had been given. Leaflets might be given either to all those on the site or just to the owners of the vehicles; if the owners were not with their vehicles, leaflets would be stuck to windscreens or posted inside empty vehicles. Despite these provisions, some officers were unsure that if a case went to court they could prove that an individual had received a direction and, as a result, were now video-recording police instructions to leave.

---

5   Several officers protested about how, when attempting to remove a group of travellers from a site, they received 'barrages' of faxes from solicitors based at particular Law Centres around the country concerning the extent of their powers and the rights of those on the site.

Along with the direction, officers would give those on the site a deadline by which to vacate the land. Prior to this point the police might make enquiries about the health and welfare of those on the site. Some officers believed that such enquiries offered opportunities for gypsies or New Age Travellers to engage in what were described as 'peaceful delaying tactics'. Whether valid or not, these involved reasons why the site could not be vacated, such as: a lack of diesel; a vehicle requiring maintenance; and an ill person or pregnant women who could not be moved[6]. The set deadline depended partly on such circumstances and although the most common time interval was 24 hours it could range from three hours to five days.

The giving of a s61 direction to leave was not always effective by itself, and the deadline could easily pass without any movement from New Age Travellers or gypsies on the site. In these circumstances the police would commonly seek to enforce the direction through a 'show of force' involving a large number of officers arriving at the site in vans. Having been threatened with arrest and the seizure of their vehicles most groups tended to move on. When faced with a particularly obstinate group the officer in charge might seek to get the group moving by making a number of token arrests or by using a breakdown truck to pull one or two vehicles onto the road. Overall, the use of s61 together with the related tactics always worked, there being no cases in the research where the police were unable to clear a site. The time taken to remove a group of trespassers depended on whether the landowner became involved and whether officers became aware of any welfare requirements of those on the site. Figures collected by the police show that the time taken to evict a group once it had been identified by officers could range from one day to seven months, with some forces clearly seeking to move trespassers on as quickly as possible.

Following the removal of the trespassers it was common for the police to urge the landowner to undertake work that would prevent further unauthorised access to the site[7]. Officers sometimes stated that they would not become involved in a future case of trespass if some attempt was not made to block access to a site. An additional way to ensure that the trespassers did not come back was to enforce the three-month ban on those directed to leave a site. However, this appeared to be applied rarely, if ever, since the task of ascertaining or proving a traveller's or gypsy's identity in court was described as 'impossible'. Vehicle registration numbers were commonly taken by officers as a record and in some cases vehicles were photographed. In addition, a visual record of those people resident on a site was sometimes obtained using video. Vehicle details could be checked on the Police National Computer and were sometimes passed on to officers in charge of police intelligence. However, information on the owner was not

---

6    Home Office Circular 45/1994 provides the police with guidance on making inquiries into the welfare of trespassers being removed from a site. This is described in detail below.

7    Courts and local authorities could also urge landowners to under take protective work to prevent further trespass.

always clear or up to date and the vehicle might be sold to another traveller or gypsy prior to its return to a site. Overall, it appeared that if a group of trespassers did return to a site officers would simply give another direction to leave rather than seek to activate the existing ban.

## Seizing vehicles (s62)

By encouraging a group to leave a site using the above tactics officers rarely needed to use s62 to seize any vehicles. However, the range of tactics officers used to clear a site partly reflected an unwillingness to use s62, with serious reservations being expressed about the organisation, expense and possibility of disorder involved in removing and storing vehicles seized from a site. Officers generally did not discount seizing vehicles, but this course of action would have to involve a very serious situation where all else had failed.

> 'If the need arose we would use s62 but the logistics would be horrendous. Think how many men with lifting equipment it would take. What are you going to do with the families? What do you do with the property inside the caravan? Where are you going to store these things?' Interviewee 40-30-09

> 'It would have to be a large disruptive group threatening violence or involving large scale damage to property, so it would have to be an extreme case. But it would be a massive job. We could do it, but it would be difficult.' Interviewee 15-30-07

> 'What do we do with all the caravans? Where do we put them? When you have impounded all the caravans, what do you do with all the people? The cost is astronomical. The organisation, the logistics of actually doing it is a nightmare, it really is. It would need a great deal of planning.' Interviewee 15-39-21

The reluctance of officers to seize vehicles could extend the battle of nerves. Here officers might give a direction to leave in the hope that the trespassers would vacate the site voluntarily, since the means to physically remove vehicles was not always available.

> 'I suppose it's a little bit of a gamble. On one hand once we've served the notice on them, we know that 99 per cent of the time they will go. So with that in mind we are reluctant to set up what amounts to a large-scale operation to remove them on the day, should they fail to go.' Interviewee 15-39-21

*'I think in the past that's what's always happened. The police have bluffed, been made to take some action and as a result got some co-operation, it's most unsatisfactory really.'* Interviewee 15-30-07

Some interviewees felt that a direction to leave should not be given if officers were not prepared to back it up with firm action as the direction could, over time, become useless.

In only one case from the current research did the police actually go ahead and seize vehicles. This involved a large group of gypsies, with an estimated 30 vehicles, who had camped on the playing fields of a grant-maintained school and, not having heard of the new provisions, were convinced the police did not have the right to remove them. The superintendent in charge of the resulting operation called for additional personnel from other divisions and contacted the local authority in order to use their vehicle pounds and possibly house those people who had their vehicles seized. Having arrived at the site in large numbers the police began removing vehicles using one of their own recovery lorries and a towing truck hired from a local garage.

Unsurprisingly, those people having their vehicles seized reacted angrily and resisted the seizure, leading to a number of arrests for assault. A total of three cars, two caravans and a large tarmacking lorry were seized. On this evidence the remaining gypsies on the playing fields decided to vacate the site. However, further disruption occurred when a group of gypsies arrived at the police vehicle pound, assaulted the officer on guard and took back their vehicles. This led to two gypsies being arrested and eventually charged, prosecuted and fined for theft, as the vehicles in the pound were legally in the police's possession. The vehicles were eventually reclaimed by the gypsies on payment of £105 per vehicle, to cover police towing and storage costs.

## Issues linked to the provisions

### The responsibilities of local authorities

An important development that reflects how certain sections of the CJPOA have been legally contested involves a judicial review carried out in August 1995[8]. This involved Wealden District Council which used ss77 and 78 of the CJPOA to remove a group of New Age Travellers in Crowborough, East Sussex. This action was challenged in the High Court, with the case centring on the welfare of a number of pregnant women either on the site when the travellers were directed to leave or arriving sometime afterwards. In what

---

8    *R* v *Wealden District Council, ex parte Wales* (1995) The Times, September 1. See also a case heard at the same time: *R* v *Lincolnshire County Council, ex parte Atkinson.*

has become known as the '*Wealden Judgement*', the local authority's removal direction and subsequent magistrates' court removal order were quashed because the local authority had failed to take into account specific sections of a Department of the Environment (DoE) circular (DoE Circular 18/94). These stated that the power to evict should not be used needlessly against gypsies and, outlined a wide range of obligations concerning the welfare of those on a site that the local authority should fulfil prior to the use of its powers[9]. This decision led to a heated debate between local authorities, their representative bodies and the DoE, with local authorities arguing that *Wealden* made the provisions given to them by the CJPOA unworkable[10].

Few officers made direct reference to *Wealden*. However, at least two forces appeared wary of using their powers as a result of this judgement. Some officers felt that its implications had fed through to New Age Travellers and gypsies, who were now choosing only to camp on local authority land and thereby avoiding the police's attentions. One officer felt that the police's ability to deal with New Age Travellers and gypsies had therefore been 'emasculated'. Another described how he had once sought to remove a disruptive group of travellers from local authority land, but the authority was concerned about fulfilling its obligations and had told him in no uncertain terms to leave them alone.

Some legal commentators have argued that *Wealden* applies to all public agencies including the police (Clements and Low-Beer, 1996). However, the obligation placed upon the police appears weaker than that borne by local authorities, with the Home Office circular accompanying the CJPOA stating that, when deciding whether to use their powers with regard to trespassers, senior officers at the scene:

> '*may wish to take account of the personal circumstances of the trespassers; for example, the presence of elderly persons, invalids, pregnant women, children and other persons whose well being may be jeopardised by a precipitate move.*' Home Office Circular 45/1994 (authors' underlining)

In general the circumstances of each case would appear to define whether and to what extent officers should make enquiries about the personal circumstances of trespassers. When serious disorder is occurring, no enquiry may be necessary. However, if time allows it would be reasonable for some enquiry to be made into the welfare of the trespassers before a direction is made.

---

9   These obligations included duties relating to the Children Act 1989 (Part III), the Housing Act 1985 (Part III) and various Education Acts, along with the need to liaise with other local authorities and with the relevant health and welfare services.

10  For a full discussion of *R v Wealden District Council, ex parte Wales* and its implications see Cragg and Low-Beer (1995).

Any concern surrounding the use of the provisions was tempered by the wide range of other powers available to officers, which could be applied according to the circumstances. Thus, the Public Order Act 1986, breach of the peace and charges of criminal damage could be used for trespass involving intimidation, harassment, disorder and damage to property. For cases of peaceful trespass various traffic legislation could be used, such as the Road Traffic Act 1988 (s34) which deals with vehicles driven without lawful authority on land not forming part of a road.

This wide range of powers meant that officers could, on occasion, legally remove trespassers from local authority property without recourse to the CJPOA's provisions. One example of this concerned a group of gypsies who had camped on a local authority car park just before Christmas 1995. Officers believed that the timing of their arrival was designed to allow them to stay for the holiday period since, with the local authority and courts shortly about to close, it appeared likely that nothing would be done before the New Year. However, while in the view of the police the site fell outside the provisions contained in the CJPOA, the trespassers had camped in a pay-and-display car park without paying and officers discovered that they therefore had the power to evict under the Road Traffic Regulation Act 1984.

## Displacement

Although the provisions could be used to clear a site of New Age Travellers and gypsies, officers commonly expressed a degree of scepticism about whether they actually solved the problem. Often the group in question would comply with a direction, only to move to another site in the local area, or, as cited in some cases, swap sites with another group.

> *'You don't solve the problem, you just solve your immediate problem on the industrial estate and it simply moves elsewhere. It doesn't solve the problem since these people go on to someone else's land.'* Interviewee 13-21-28

> *'They moved on but they just moved to the other side of the road. And I served notices on the other side of the road. I have chased one group now for over a year and I have served eight lots of notices on them, from one bit of land to another bit of land, to another bit of land to another bit of land. So you just chase them around.'* Interviewee 37-12-26

> *'The Act's a curate's egg – it's good in parts. It is excellent to move them, but you have no power to stop them from going to the field next door.'* Interviewee 40-30-09

In addition, directing trespassers off a site could lead to immediate difficulties since the size of the group and the roadworthiness of some vehicles could lead to serious traffic problems. Some officers believed the issue of trespass could be solved by the provision of more legal sites for travellers and gypsies. Others suggested that a change in social security regulations to exclude these groups from eligibility for benefit would drive them from their way of life.

The issue of displacement has to be viewed along side the relevant CJPOA provisions which were not designed to reduce the problem of trespassing on land, but to deal with trespassers who become a serious nuisance. Under these provisions only groups of trespassers who are consistently disruptive, destructive or above a certain size could be repeatedly moved on. In addition, the immediate possibility of displacement could be dealt with by a landowner or local authourity under civil law which allows court orders seeking possession to be extended to other sites as well as that being camped if there is reason to believe that these too are in danger of encampment. One effect of the CJPOA, reflected in the interviews, was that some travellers and gypsies *were now more* likely to travel and camp in smaller groups than before in order to avoid the attentions of the authorities. In addition these groups may become more static, deciding to stay in illegal but informally tolerated sites rather than risk being moved on.

## Use of provisions, and number of cautions and prosecutions

Police figures for 1995 show that officers across 15 forces in England and Wales gave a direction to leave land (s61) 67 times and that there were no cases in which the police seized vehicles (s62). The use of s61 varied widely from force to force, with one force using it 16 times, while the majority used this power either once or twice. The number of people being directed from land in each of the instances also varied widely, ranging from three to 46. The number of motorised vehicles and caravans evicted ranged from six to 52, with the average number evicted being around a dozen.

Official statistics are only collected for cautions, prosecutions and convictions under s61. Perhaps reflecting the police's success in enforcing s61, these show that prosecutions were rare, with only four occurring in 1995 and again in 1996 (see Table 2.1). The three convictions in 1995 all led to fines, the average amount being £100. No prosecutions led to a conviction during 1996. Cautioning was relatively common and may reflect difficulties relating to prosecutions. Figures are also available for s39 of the Public Order Act 1986 (the power which s61 replaced). These figures cover the first three years of s39's existence (1987, 1988 and 1989) and show a higher number of court actions compared with s61. During these three years there were no cautions, and the average number of prosecutions was 13. In 1989 a total of 19 prosecutions resulted in seven convictions involving an average fine of £150.

### Table 2.1: Cautions and court proceedings for failure to leave land as directed/ returning as trespasser within three months (s61)

|  |  | Cautions | Prosecutions | Convictions |
|---|---|---|---|---|
| Failure to leave/returning | 1995 | 5 | 4 | 3 |
|  | 1996 | 13 | 4 | 0 |

## Key points

- The CJPOA provisions relating to trespass on land have been applied to both New Age Travellers and gypsies, although forces' practice in relation to the latter varied. While some had used the provisions to direct gypsies from land, others felt the legislation had not been designed for use against gypsies and therefore did not apply it to this group. Other forces only used the provisions in 'extreme cases' and instead worked with the local authority and gypsies to minimise disturbances caused by trespass on land.

- The identification of an illegal encampment usually led to some discussion between the police, local authority and landowner. Police action tended to depend on whether there was any evidence of damage to land or property and whether the landowner was capable of removing the trespassers using a civil law remedy.

- Once the police became involved, a battle of nerves tended to develop between officers and those on the site, escalating through a number of stages before full use of the CJPOA's provisions.

- Directions to trespassers to leave a site always led to the site being cleared. However, a direction was not always effective by itself since a large number of officers sometimes had to attend the site, with the associated threat of arrest and seizure of vehicles leading groups to move on. The making of token arrests and the towing of one or two vehicles onto the highway usually led to more obstinate groups vacating the site.

- Difficulties recording the identities of trespassers meant that officers rarely had sufficient evidence to prove that someone had returned to a site after being directed away. As a result, if a group of trespassers was thought to have returned to a site within three months officers would simply give another direction to leave rather than make an arrest.

- Officers were very wary about using their powers under s62 to seize vehicles due to the related organisation and expense. While not totally discounting the seizure of vehicles, officers generally felt that the situation would have to be very serious to warrant this form of action.

- Few officers made direct reference to the 'Wealden Judgement' on the welfare obligations facing local authorities in relation to people living on illegal encampments. However, some felt that this judgement meant that New Age Travellers and gypsies were now more likely to camp on local authority land to avoid the police's attentions.

- Officers stated that the use of the provisions could lead to New Age Travellers and gypsies simply moving to other illegal sites thereby displacing the problem.

- Section 61 was used by police officers 67 times in 1995, with these instances varying widely in the numbers of people and vehicles evicted. Prosecutions under the provisions were very rare. Only four prosecutions occurred under s61 in both 1995 and 1996, with no convictions in the latter year.

# 3 Raves

This chapter examines the measures in the CJPOA designed to deal with large, unlicensed parties called 'raves'. Emerging during the late 1980s, raves soon gained a great deal of publicity due to the disturbances and activities linked to such events. These could include loud music being played for long periods late at night, severe traffic congestion, the consumption of illegal drugs and public disorder[1]. Prior to the CJPOA, the police had no statutory powers to intervene in a rave if a private landowner had given permission for such a gathering to take place, the only available powers being those under common law breach of the peace. Local authorities could deal with a noise nuisance under the Environmental Protection Act 1990. However, they were not always equipped to act quickly enough to prevent a rave from proceeding. The perceived lack of sufficient powers led to the inclusion in the CJPOA of provisions giving the police powers to: stop unlicensed raves that are either being set up or are already in progress; seize sound equipment; and redirect people on their way to an event.

## The CJPOA provisions

The CJPOA provisions apply only to particular kinds of event, due to the very specific way in which 'raves' have been defined. Under the Act a rave is defined as an unlicensed gathering on land in the open air of 100 or more persons (whether or not trespassers) at which amplified music is played with or without intermissions during the night. The volume, duration and the time at which the music is played must be likely to cause serious distress to the inhabitants of the locality (CJPOA s63(1)). Perhaps because of the types of music played at raves the Act defines 'music' as including 'sounds wholly or predominantly characterised by the emission of a succession of repetitive beats' (s63(1)(b)).

While commentators have raised questions about the definitions of 'land', 'open air' and 'serious distress' (see Card and Ward, 1994), the aim of the provisions is clearly that they should be used in very particular instances (i.e. to limit large, unauthorised music events held outdoors and causing problems for local residents). They were not designed for indoor parties or

---

1   One police response to this new phenomenon was the creation of a 'Pay Party Unit' responsible for collecting and disseminating information on forthcoming raves to forces across England and Wales.

licensed clubs that may disturb residents, or for unlicensed dance events held in isolated places that cause no serious problems for local inhabitants

The CJPOA creates three police powers to be used in relation to 'raves'.

### i    Powers to remove people attending or preparing for a rave (s63)

Under s63 a police officer of the rank of at least superintendent can direct people to leave the site of a rave, taking any vehicles or other property with them. Unlike other powers in the CJPOA to direct people to leave private land, s63 does not have to be exercised by a senior officer at the scene; instead, the direction can be issued by a superintendent at headquarters and communicated to officers at the site of the rave. Furthermore, the senior officer does not have to wait for numbers of people at a rave to build up before giving a s63 direction. A direction to leave land can be given only when a senior officer reasonably believes that:

- two or more people are making preparations for a rave;

- ten or more are present waiting for a rave to begin; or

- ten or more are attending such a rave which is in progress.

Under this power a person commits an offence if, having received a direction, he or she fails to leave the land as soon as reasonably practicable, or enters the land again within seven days.

### ii    Powers of entry and seizure of sound equipment (s64)

Under s64 police constables can be authorised to enter land if an officer of the rank of superintendent or above reasonably believes that there is a rave occurring which would justify a s63 direction. Furthermore, officers can seize or remove vehicles or sound equipment if they are not removed following a s63 direction or if a trespasser returns to the site with such items within seven days of being ordered from the land.

### iii    The power to stop people proceeding to a rave (s65)

Having sought to halt a rave using a s63 direction, officers have the power to deal with those hoping to attend the event. Under s65 officers can stop anyone within a five-mile radius of the site who they reasonably believe is travelling to the gathering and direct them not to proceed to the rave. Having been directed away, it is an offence not to comply.

Offences under ss63 and 65 are summary only. The maximum punishment under s63 is three months' imprisonment or a fine of up to £2,500, or both. The maximum punishment under s65 is a fine of up to £1,000.

## Policing raves under the CJPOA

### Raves prior to the CJPOA

The raves of the late 1980s and early 1990s were described as being difficult to police due to their size and unpredictability. On some occasions officers were aware that a rave was going to occur but did not know the location. As a result large numbers of young people had been tracked over great distances and across police force boundaries. On other occasions the police were forced to respond to a large rave occurring at a particular location without any warning. Officers had attempted to manage one particular rave by surrounding it, but had failed since the gathering was too large; others had been forced to let ravers onto a prospective rave site as there was no other way to control them. In one instance officers found themselves heavily outnumbered by a hostile crowd and on another were attacked by security guards employed by the event's organisers. More general problems identified included: serious traffic congestion; roads blocked by abandoned vehicles; destroyed farm crops; disturbance caused by traffic noise and music; and harm caused to the land by the discarding of rubbish and drug paraphernalia, and a lack of sanitation.

Before the CJPOA, officers commonly used common law breach of the peace in connection with raves. Other public order powers and illegal drugs legislation were also used, while sound systems were seized using the Local Government (Miscellaneous Provisions) Act 1982. Legislation concerning entertainment licences and public nuisance was also employed on occasion. How well these powers fitted the circumstances was debatable. As one officer stated:

> 'Most police forces involved used legislation on occasions inappropriately. Police forces were forced to make it up as they went along.' Interviewee 36-31-25

A common theme in interviews with officers was that by the time the CJPOA provisions were available illegal raves had become a rare phenomenon compared with the late-1980s. Some commentators see this as being due to increasingly successful police tactics and the liberalising of licensing laws, with the result that rave organisers and those attending moved to and became integrated in the mainstream entertainment sector (see Collin, 1997).

The illegal raves focused on in this chapter fell into two categories. The first involved rather modest versions of the raves held during the late-1980s, taking place in rural sites but organised and run by groups from urban areas. The second category involved much larger events that came to prominence after the wave of raves during the late-1980s and early-1990s. These involved groups of New Age Travellers coming together (usually in the summer months) and holding raves on their large encampments.

## Different police approaches

How officers approached the policing of an unlicensed rave principally depended on exactly when they came to hear about the event. In a number of cases officers were informed of a rave through telephone calls from local residents reporting heavy traffic or loud music. If, by this stage, sound equipment had reached the site and people were arriving, officers felt, for reasons outlined below, that their options were very restricted. As a result, a great deal of value was placed on intelligence that warned officers of a forthcoming rave.

> 'From experience you need the intelligence first, because if you've got the intelligence that something is going to happen you can look out for it and you can nip it in the bud straight away.' Interviewee 07-40-33

This intelligence could come from within their own force, other constabularies, or the Northern and Southern Intelligence Units. The actual information might be drawn from promotional flyers or stickers handed out on the street or at club venues, the internet, or via word of mouth. In one case a force had a week's advance notice of an impending rave. However, in some cases intelligence only told officers that a rave was occurring on a particular day, without pinpointing the exact time or location. Any telephone lines providing information on a rave might be monitored in an attempt to ascertain the site and arrive before the ravers. Without this information officers could find themselves following a convoy of ravers to a site and arriving only after large numbers had built up.

Depending on the amount of notice received about a rave, officers could choose between stopping or containing it. The way in which the CJPOA provisions were used depended upon which option was chosen, with the following two cases highlighting this point.

### Option one: stopping the rave

In April 1995 a northern police force found that an illegal rave had been organised to take place on a Saturday night on the site of a quarry set in some woodland. Officers had been informed of the rave shortly before it was to begin by the quarry's caretaker who had found posters and leaflets at the quarry advertising the event. The police found more posters advertising the rave and giving directions to the site along roads in the area, while two officers arriving at the quarry found a number of people, believed to be the organisers of the event, and a number of vehicles containing food, drinks and sound equipment.

The superintendent based at divisional headquarters believed the event constituted a rave under the CJPOA and that serious distress was likely to be caused to people living in a row of houses 100 yards from the site. A sergeant at the quarry was then authorised to use s63 to direct the people organising the rave immediately away from the site. The organisers initially ignored the direction and were described as 'very argumentative'. The sergeant then threatened to arrest them, although, as he later admitted, this would have been difficult considering the two officers attending were heavily outnumbered. However, this threat, along with attempts by the officers to physically guide people from the site, led the organisers to start moving the sound equipment, food and drink back to their vehicles. Officers considered seizing the sound equipment, but the option was dismissed due to the lack of personnel at the scene.

As officers arranged the removal of the organisers' equipment from the site, people began to arrive for the rave and protested about the police preventing the event. These people were also directed to leave the quarry under s63. Eventually the officers cleared the site of people and then blocked off the road from which it could be accessed. Officers then remained on duty at the site for several hours, with the authority to use s65 to direct people not to proceed towards it. Three convoys consisting of approximately 15 cars each were directed away during this time. These were described as coming from the region's towns and cities. At the same time officers patrolled the surrounding area to ensure that the organisers did not set up somewhere else. Officers were also sent to the pubs in local villages in case there were any public order problems.

### Option two: containing the rave

According to the police, a large rave, known as 'The Mother of all Raves' was planned to occur during July 1995 in one of three possible locations in Britain. Early police action at one site in the west of England led the organisers to relocate to another in a neighbouring county. The first indication officers had that a rave was to occur in their area was on a Saturday afternoon through calls from local residents reporting a group of New Age Travellers beginning to occupy a piece of common land. By the time police had arrived in numbers, around 30 vehicles of various types were parked across the common, including a lorry containing sound equipment.

Because of the number of New Age Travellers and ravers already on the common, senior officers decided against using s63 to clear the site. As one senior officer stated, those on the site 'had clearly communicated to us that any order to remove them would be strongly resisted. Directing them off the common was only going to cause confrontation'. To have gone ahead with such a direction would have been 'tactically difficult, offering a low chance of success, and being likely to result in injuries both to officers and those attending the event. Even threatening the use of s63 was discounted' as this was unlikely to have had any effect and, since it could not be enforced, would only have resulted in undermining the police's authority.

Instead, officers decided upon a policy of containment using s65[2]. Those on the common were therefore left to 'get on with it' while the police directed their resources at limiting the numbers of people actually attending the event. Approximately 50 officers had been called from across the force to deal with the event, with others on standby. Six stop-checks were created and s65 was used to direct away those hoping to attend the rave. This was aided by the low number of access roads into the area. Officers were busy turning a large number of people away from the rave for the first few hours, with potential attendees soon declining as it became clear there was no access to the rave. The police presence remained throughout Saturday evening, was gradually reduced during the night and built up again the following day, by which time the rave was over. The New Age Travellers were said to have left the area over the next four days. The overall strategy was judged a success by officers since the event never reached its potential size and the internet was 'buzzing with a lot of very rude comments about the police and what they had done'. Summing up this type of situation one officer stated:

> 'Once you get those sorts of numbers I don't know anyone who would go in. You've just got to contain it and try to keep the locals happy, and make it as uncomfortable as possible for those on the site.' Interviewee 01–13–06

## Definitional issues in the use of the provisions

Officers gave examples of cases where the nature of the event meant that it clearly fell outside the CJPOA's definition of a 'rave', including events either in enclosed buildings, in remote areas or involving small groups of people. However, other cases were less clear cut. The best example of this concerned a large rave which was to be held on a New Age Travellers' site in the Midlands, made up of approximately 100 vehicles. Despite believing that the rave was being organised from within the site the police had little hard

---

2    The use of s65 to direct people away from a rave without the use of s63 is discussed below.

evidence that people there were making preparations for a rave. Distinguishing those people who might be organising a rave from the other 300-400 people living on the site was described as impossible. Furthermore, no sound equipment suitable for a large rave had reached the location. It was also open to question whether any rave would actually be occurring on 'land' within the meaning of the Act, as the New Age Travellers' camp could be defined as a residential caravan site. In addition, the site happened to be on a Roman road known as the Ermin Way, which made its status as 'land' even more ambiguous. Because of these issues senior officers decided against directing people from the site using s63 and, as in the previous example, directed people away from the area using s65. The police operation lasted three days, with 70 officers on duty at its height. Several thousand people were turned away.

The definition of 'buildings' was also an issue in policing raves. One such event was held at an equestrian centre and involved a building which was partly open to the air. Officers were concerned about whether the building's design meant that it fell outside the legal definition of a 'rave' since, according to the Act, such an event had to occur in the open air. They finally decided not to use the provisions because of this question. Other officers voiced concerns about the status of a large marquee. None had policed a rave involving such a structure, but, as one officer stated, such an event 'would not be big enough to cause us any bother'.

The impact of definitional issues went beyond affecting the use of the provisions at specific events. One officer stated that his force had initially had a policy of not using any of the provisions until the meanings of various terms were more fully understood. Definitional issues with regard to the provisions are only likely to be resolved through court actions and judicial decisions about what terms such as 'land' and 'open air' include and exclude. When such issues arose and led to the provisions not being used, officers either resorted to other public order powers or came to a negotiated agreement with the rave organisers to minimise the impact of the event on local inhabitants.

## Practical issues in the use of the provisions

Officers raised a number of issues resulting from their use of the provisions. Some were concerned that they could be challenged over whether they had taken 'reasonable steps' to ensure that a direction to leave the site of a rave had been communicated to those present. Under the CJPOA individual constables can communicate to those at the scene a senior officer's direction to leave a rave. However, when dispersing large groups, attendees may still deny that they have been told to leave and may refuse to move. As it would be impossible to record each constable telling attendees to leave some forces had video-taped the senior officer giving a direction through a set of loud speakers, to provide at least some evidence that people had been told.

Under the CJPOA provisions it is an offence for a person to return to the site of a rave within seven days of having been directed to leave. There was no evidence that anyone had been arrested or prosecuted for this offence. This was due to a number of reasons, the main one being that if someone complied with a direction to leave a rave the police were unlikely to have recorded any personal details, thereby making any alleged return to the site difficult to prove. Personal details tended to be taken only from organisers: for example, when they were found preparing for a rave. Therefore, if someone returned to the site of a rave it was likely that they would simply be directed away again rather than arrested for breach of the original direction.

The power to seize sound equipment was also rarely used because practical and legal considerations made this problematic. Where such equipment had not yet arrived at a site, the police would seek to intercept it at the earliest possible moment. Since the rave provisions do not deal with equipment in transit, the police looked to offences such as breach of the peace and conspiracy to cause a public nuisance[3], or sought to turn away from the rave any vehicle carrying the equipment using s65. As officers stated:

*'If they attempted to drive on to the site with equipment they would be turned back like everyone else. But we wouldn't allow them on the site just to give us the power to seize the equipment.'* Interviewee 01-25-38

*'We knew if we could stop the gear getting through then we wouldn't have a problem.'* Interviewee 07-05-16

If the sound equipment had already arrived at the site and the rave had begun, senior officers were unlikely to attempt any seizure as such a foray at night by officers with large numbers of ravers in attendance would not be worth the attendant risks. As one officer stated:

*'Before you get hoards of ravers then it is not impossible. But my best guess is that we had possibly 5,000 to 6,000 people turn up during the course of Friday night. If they had got on site then the seizing of equipment would be impossible.'* Interviewee 23-19-49

---

3    Some officers expressed concern about how appropriate these powers were. The use of conspiracy to cause a public nuisance was described as 'frightening' and involving 'some loose legal ground' since no public nuisance had actually occurred.

Usually when officers arrived before a rave had started, rather than using s64 to seize equipment they tended to get the organisers to remove it, keeping the threat of seizure in reserve[4]. In only one case did equipment fall into the police's hands. This was mainly by default when, after a rave had been broken up, the organiser left with his own sound equipment, informing the police that they could have the hired set of equipment along with the hired van.

The creation of an exclusion zone around the rave also could pose some difficulties. Typically this involved placing various vehicle check-points at certain points in the surrounding area. If these were sited too far from the rave they could involve considerable numbers of officers as well as cause serious disruption to traffic, including local inhabitants. However, if sited too close they might be ineffective. In one case, check-points were close enough to a rave for those already attending to call to those being turned back to ignore the police cordon, and this led to some disorder. In another case, those seeking to attend avoided check-points by driving through fields, thereby damaging crops and risking a fire among the dry wheat and hay.

Another issue in the use of the provisions concerned officers' misunderstandings of the legislation. In one case officers simply confused the different provisions and used s63 not to direct people already at the site to leave but, instead, to direct people travelling to the rave away from it. A more serious misunderstanding involved a number of raves where commanding officers decided to contain rather than stop the event. They therefore did not apply s63 to clear the site but used s65 to prevent other people attending. When asked about this the officers appeared unaware that, according to the legislation, s65 can only be used in regard to a rave 'to which a direction under section 63(2) is in force' (s65(1) of CJPOA). The legislation therefore states that the police cannot direct people away from a rave without having first directed those already in attendance to leave[5]. That these provisions have to be used in conjunction with each other, and are not free-standing, appeared not to be clear to a number of officers interviewed.

## Assessments

The creation of new police powers and offences is unlikely to be met with hostility from police officers, and, unsurprisingly, those who had exercised the provisions were generally positive about them. Officers felt that they had led to a more effective response from the police:

---

4   An associated problem here was that, having complied with a s63 direction to leave, the organisers might simply move to another site and set their equipment up again. To counter this possibility officers would follow the vehicle carrying the equipment once it had left the site to ensure that it departed from the area

5   This is also the case for s64, since the seizure of sound equipment can only take place once a s63 direction to leave the rave has been applied.

*'Certainly it's effective. We knew we had to stop it for public safety reasons and without that particular Act and section [s63] we would have been struggling to knock it on the head effectively.'* Interviewee 07-28-14

*'I mean s63 is a winner. Once we clarified we could apply it and we were quite satisfied that we could apply it in these circumstances it worked like a dream.'* Interviewee 07-05-16

*'Excellent, excellent, they cater for everything we want. It's there, it's plain common-sense.'* Interviewee 07-40-33

In order to examine the extent to which the provisions had made a difference interviewees were asked what they would have done if the powers and offences had not existed when they policed a particular event. Only one officer felt that without the provisions his task would have been more difficult.

*'Had I not had that power how would I have got them off the private land to start with? If I'd said, "You're not allowed to be here because it's private land", they wouldn't have cared less, they were intent on stopping there. There would have been no action I could have taken to follow what I'd been telling them.'* Interviewee 07-40-33

Other officers stated that they would have looked to alternative powers to allow them to stop or contain the rave. These included local bylaws, the Public Order Act 1986, laws concerning criminal damage, environmental health laws and, most commonly, breach of the peace. However, officers raised concerns about how appropriate these powers were for the circumstances.

*'We would have probably struggled because we would have been stopping people and using common law powers to prevent a breach of the peace. Those laws can be difficult to back up in a court of law, when a breach of the peace doesn't really take place.'* Interviewee 07-05-16

*'I think we would have probably stretched the common law powers of public nuisance and used them to turn people away.'* Interviewee 23-19-49

The extent to which broadly the same tactics would have been followed, despite not having the CJPOA's provisions, was underlined by officers describing that if all else failed they would have fallen back on the 'Ways and

Means Act'. Here, officers lacking any clear legal powers would rely on the general authority attached to their position and seek to resolve a situation through a mixture of negotiation and persuasion. A result of the provisions contained in the CJPOA therefore appears to be that officers now police raves from a much stronger legal position.

*'It now gives us the ability to do what we were doing probably before, I wouldn't say illegally, but we were misusing or using inappropriately on occasions common law, or our understanding of what common law is.'* Interviewee 36-31-25

*'If we have a problem we've got the full backing of the law to go ahead and do it. We're not worried about whether we are exactly right with the law, have we done this with the law, have we done that. It's bang on, the legislation is there for what we need.'* Interviewee 07-40-33

## Use of provisions, and number of cautions and prosecutions

Very few people were arrested using the CJPOA's rave provisions, partly because most people tended to comply with police directions rather than face the consequences. As one officer stated: 'Nine times of ten the mere threat of arrest solves the problem'. Furthermore, to have made arrests would have drawn police personnel away from the event with at least two officers being needed to deal with every person arrested. Such a course of action would have gone against the police's main objective, which was to regain public order by taking control of the event, stopping the music and dispersing the ravers, or at least reducing the extent of disturbance.

Figures collected by the police show that during 1995 the rave provisions were used as follows.

- On nine occasions a senior officer authorised that people should be directed away from a rave; this occurred in eight forces across England and Wales, with numbers directed away under this power ranging from 12 to 50 people.

- On one occasion sound equipment was seized by the police (s64).

- On 32 occasions a senior officer authorised that those seeking to attend a rave should be directed away under s65; the numbers involved ranged from 45 to 500 people.

A high level of compliance among those given directions by officers meant few cautions and court proceedings resulted. Official figures show that there were no prosecutions for failing to comply with a direction not to proceed towards a rave (s65) during the first two years of this power's existence. During 1995 no one had any formal action taken against them for failing to leave the site of a rave (s63), while during 1996 seven people were prosecuted under this power, of whom four were convicted. Of these, two received fines of around £250 and two received conditional discharges.

### Table 3.1: Cautions and court proceedings under s63 CJPOA

|  |  | Cautions | Prosecutions | Convictions |
|---|---|---|---|---|
| Failure to leave/returning | 1995 | 0 | 0 | 0 |
|  | 1996 | 1 | 7 | 4 |

## Key points

- The way in which the CJPOA's rave measures were used principally depended on when the police came to hear about the holding of a rave. If informed early enough officers might try to stop the rave by directing those already at the site away (using s63) and ensuring those travelling to the event were turned back (using s65). When a rave was in progress officers might 'contain' the event through the use of stop-checks and by instructing those arriving to attend not to proceed any further (using s65).

- Various raves had raised issues about the wording of the provisions. Officers had experienced problems establishing that people were 'making preparations for a rave' and what the terms 'land' and 'open air' included and excluded. In at least one force officers had refrained from using the rave measures until these terms had been clarified through court actions and judicial decisions.

- The power to arrest someone for returning to a rave, after having been directed away by officers was rarely, if ever, used. Those initially complying with officers' directions seldom had their personal details taken, thereby making an alleged return to a rave hard to prove. If someone was thought to have returned it was likely that they would simply be directed away again.

- The power to seize sound equipment was rarely used since officers tended to get those responsible for such equipment to remove it when clearing a rave site. When sound equipment was being driven to a rave officers would seek to apprehend it using other powers rather than allowing it to arrive at the site and then seizing it. When a rave was in full progress officers rejected the possibility of entering the site and seizing the equipment because of the dangers facing them.

- Under the provisions officers can only stop people proceeding to a rave using s65 when a direction under s63 is in force. However some officers were unclear about this and had used s65 on occasions when s63 had not been applied.

- Officers were generally positive about the CJPOA provisions, which were seen as allowing them to police raves from a stronger legal position than in the past.

- Most people tended to comply with the directions when they were issued. A high level of compliance meant a low number of court proceedings, with only seven people being prosecuted under s63 during 1996 and none under s65.

# 4 Aggravated trespass

This chapter is divided into two parts, reflecting how the measures concerning aggravated trespass have been applied to two different public order situations. One is the activities of animal rights protesters. The other is environmental protest and particularly the conflict surrounding the development of the Newbury bypass.

## The CJPOA provisions

Sections 68 and 69 of the CJPOA are aimed at trespassers who seek to intimidate or disrupt people engaged in a lawful activity on land. These measures created a great deal of controversy during their passage through Parliament since they determine the line between two freedoms – to pursue a lawful activity and to express an opinion (Card and Ward, 1994). The measures were aimed primarily at the actions of hunt saboteurs[1] and more generally at animal rights protesters seeking to disrupt or obstruct activities such as the shooting of game, horse-racing and angling (see Hansard, Vol 235, col 29). Although not specifically mentioned during the CJPOA's passage through Parliament, the measures' emphasis on lawful activity on land means that they also extend to certain forms of environmental protest. Their application with regard to protesters opposing the building of particular roads has, in fact, been one of the most important areas in which they have been applied.

### Aggravated trespass

In order to deal with the activities of protesters the CJPOA created a new offence, that of aggravated trespass. Section 68 of the CJPOA defines the offence as involving trespassing on land in the open air and doing anything intended to:

- intimidate people and deter them from engaging in a lawful activity;

- obstruct a lawful activity; or

---

1     Previous concern about disorder at hunts led to a 1992 Home Office circular providing guidance on these events (Home Office Circular 11/1992). Prepared in consultation with ACPO, the circular outlined the role of the police at hunts, and provided advice on liaison, intelligence, the policing of meets and the control of dogs.

- disrupt a lawful activity (s68(1)).

Section 68(2) defines an activity as lawful when it can be undertaken on the land without the people involved committing an offence or trespassing.

### *Direction to leave*

Section 69 of the CJPOA corresponds to ss61 and 63, since it provides the police with the power to direct people to leave land. Under s69 the senior officer present may order people to leave land if he/she believes:

- they are committing, have committed or intend to commit an offence of aggravated trespass on land in the open air; or

- that two or more people are trespassing on land in the open air and are present there with the common purpose of intimidating persons so as to deter them from engaging in a lawful activity or of obstructing or disrupting a lawful activity (s69(1)).

An offence occurs if, having been given a direction, a person fails to leave the land or returns to the land within seven days, having been directed away. It is a defence if those arrested can show that, at the time of arrest for breach of the direction, they were not trespassing or had a reasonable excuse for not leaving or returning (s69(4)).

Both aggravated trespass and failing to leave land are summary offences. The maximum penalty for either offence is three months' imprisonment or a fine of up to £2,500, or both.

## Part one: fox hunting

To understand the impact of the CJPOA's provisions some background is necessary about the policing of fox hunts.

## Hunts and saboteurs

The fox hunting season usually begins in November and continues until April. It is preceded by 'cub hunting' which commences after the harvest in late August or September and involves young and inexperienced hounds being introduced to the pack and trained to follow the scent of the fox. Officers interviewed policed areas containing between one and six fox hunts. These events occasionally roamed into different police divisions and across force boundary lines. Officers could have hunts taking place within their area several times a week or just half a dozen times during a season. The size of each hunt varied according to whether a particular 'meet' was held on a weekday, weekend, or on a public holiday, such as Boxing Day. Estimates of attendance therefore ranged from 15 to 100 riders and from five to over 100 hunt followers. Attending fox hunts was not seen as a popular form of police work. Policing such events was described as a 'pain' due to the necessary devotion of resources and preparation time, the criticism received from the various groups involved, and the operational difficulties faced on the day.

Hunts may have a regular group of saboteurs attend, whose numbers can be swelled by the attendance of saboteur groups from outside the area. Numbers of saboteurs attending hunts therefore varied widely, with police estimates ranging from as few as four to as many as several hundred when the hunt had been targeted for a specially organised 'mass sab'. Clearly, some hunts were the focus of greater saboteur activity than others, with officers reporting that on average a dozen saboteurs regularly attended their local hunts. Others gave much higher average figures of, for example, 27 and 80[2]. In addition, saboteurs might visit more than one hunt in a day.

The variation in numbers attending, while making policing unpredictable, reflected how the element of surprise is a central feature in much 'sabbing'. Sabbing usually either seeks to take the foxhounds out of the control of the hunt or to distract them away from any foxes. This is attempted through: the blowing of horns; the use of anti-scent sprays; the laying of false trails; halloaing (whistling, shouting and screaming); the playing of tapes of foxhounds in full cry; and the cracking of whips. However, saboteurs were also described as committing acts of intimidation, violence and vandalism. Hunt members and followers could be threatened, verbally abused and assaulted, while cars, kennels and other hunt and farm property could be seriously damaged. Described by officers as 'professional protesters', 'the great unwashed' and like 'football hooligans', police opinions varied on the organisation and knowledge of saboteurs. The more sophisticated saboteurs were said to use radio scanners to monitor police broadcasts and mobile phones to communicate with each other.

An important point of contact for the police was the Master of Foxhounds (MFH), primarily responsible for organising and running each hunt. Some level of liaison between officers and an MFH was usually required, since this person has overall responsibility for the behaviour of the hunt's mounted followers, as well as dictating the area to be hunted and choosing the particular places to be visited. Levels of co-operation clearly varied, with some officers finding the relationship to be strained. Particular tensions

---

2    Estimates of saboteurs attending may be inflated by the inclusion of members of the League Against Cruel Sports who were described by one officer as the hunts 'official opposition'. As well as lawfully protesting against the hunt this group may monitor it in case any unlawful actions take place.

could centre upon the level of policing being provided for a hunt[3], and officers' approach to saboteurs. Criticism of the police by members of the hunt are described in more detail at the end of this section.

Hunt stewards seek to protect the hunt from saboteurs and other protesters and are encouraged by the British Field Sports Society. Ranging from local farmworkers to ex-soldiers and professional security guards, they may offer their services for no cost or require payment. In order for stewards to be used, an MFH must have permission to act as the 'agent' for the landowner or occupier over whose land the hunt will pass. On the day of the hunt stewards are under the control of the MFH or a representative who may be on foot. Stewards are legally entitled under common law to ask trespassing saboteurs to leave private land and to use reasonable force to remove them if they refuse to comply. Police officers' views on stewards were usually negative, since their use was viewed as leading to an escalation of the violence and disorder surrounding the hunt.

> *'One or two stewards were coming along who I think were worse than the sabs. We had to tell the master of hounds that we weren't too happy with them. They were no more than glorified thugs.'*
> Interviewee 13-24-20
>
> *'They can't just be allowed to run around unchecked as vigilantes.'*
> Interviewee 01-20-48
>
> *'Luckily the hunt has stopped using stewards. Really they were thugs, they were bouncers.'* Interviewee 38-02-37

Only in two areas did officers express a positive attitude towards stewards. In one, officers had been involved in the training of stewards in an attempt to reduce the problems surrounding their use. In another area a group of professional security guards had been employed which, although proving expensive for the hunt, had been viewed as a success by officers. Stewards were not used by all the hunts in the research, with some having experimented in their use and decided against their future deployment (for reasons outlined below).

Linked to the stewards were the hunt followers, who pursue the hunt on foot and in vehicles. These could amount to over 100 people at popular meets and, like stewards, could be involved in violence and disorder. On some occasions 'militant' hunt followers were so aggressive that saboteurs were reported to have looked to the police for protection. Again, officers described hunt followers as being as much trouble as the saboteurs. The behaviour of certain followers led, in some instances, to officers asking the

---

3    Some MFHs were described as 'demanding' the attendance of several officers for mid-week hunts which were viewed as a low priority by the police.

MFH to ensure that particular people did not attend again. Another group that could be involved in disorder were the mounted members of the hunt, known as 'the field', who had been known to ride at, or whip, saboteurs and protesters[4].

Officers might have to deal with violent disorder between saboteurs and any of the above groups. Various claims and counterclaims were made by these groups concerning incidents alleged to have occurred when officers were not present. More general disorder could occur between groups, including verbal abuse, pushing, intimidation and the vandalising of vehicles. During a hunt officers could face criticism from both saboteurs and those associated with the hunt for not dealing with alleged offences occurring within their presence or elsewhere. MFHs and others involved in the hunts could be especially critical of officers who, in their view, were not enforcing the law and protecting a lawful activity. Officers described how those associated with the hunt; 'always feel we could do more'...; 'feel the police should be more on their side'...; and accuse officers of 'not doing their job by failing to arrest sabs'...

The introduction of the CJPOA's provisions was said by officers to have led to high expectations about the future policing of saboteurs. One officer described how, in attempting to control expectations, he had explained to his local hunt organisers that the CJPOA gave police 'powers but not necessarily duties and they would be treated in that way'. However, officers had faced criticism for not using the provisions as much as those involved in the hunt believed they could.

> *'We've had it where the hunt has complained to the chief constable saying: "Aggravated trespass was committed and your officers did not use their powers".'* Interviewee 31-04-45

Relations were perhaps most strained where officers and saboteurs had entered into agreements. These cases are dealt with below.

## The difficulty of policing hunts

The extent to which the CJPOA provisions were used rested heavily on officers' pre-existing practices in relation to hunts. These practices were shaped by how officers resolved the central difficulty of the unpredictability of policing these events. Public order policing invariably involves a degree of unpredictability, but in the policing of fox hunts the element of surprise deliberately used by saboteurs exacerbated this and meant that officers were never sure when or where disorder might occur.

---

4    Field Master, Huntsman and Whipper-ins are other titles and roles for mounted members of the hunt, while the Terrierman works on foot and is responsible for digging a fox out when it 'goes to ground' or putting the terriers in to flush it out.

*'What we don't know is which hunt they are normally going to go to. I mean you've got three or four hunts all over the county. We don't know where the sabs are going to go, or if they are going to go to more than one. We have to wait until they've turned up at the hunt which is rather too late.'* Interviewee 01-20-48

*'If the sabs turn up en masse and the situation starts then it is almost impossible to recover. We cannot put out enough manpower to cover the hunt over such a wide area, through fields and country lanes. With low visibility of what's going on, we can't have the resources of manpower to control or regain control of what's going on.'* Interviewee 13-06-10

A commanding officer might therefore decide on how many officers would be required to police a hunt without being sure whether these might be too many, too few or just adequate on the day. This, of course, could happen in other areas of public order policing. However, while in urban areas further and immediate support could be called upon, the geographical remoteness and inaccessibility of much hunting country meant that the chances of any effective support arriving in time were extremely low. Commanding officers were therefore forced to police hunts in the knowledge that the police already there would have to deal with any disorder by themselves.

*'But the timing is the essence, I mean the trouble is if you haven't got the officers to deal with it there and then. Normally by the time you bring them in the trouble's over and the saboteurs have disappeared - it's ever so difficult.'* Interviewee 13-06-10

*'When you start getting officers in on reserve you've to bring officers in from all over the county. It doesn't matter where the hunt is, they could come from anywhere. And by the time they end up in some backwater, they haven't got a clue where they are. It takes about two hours to get the extra manpower from other stations.'* Interviewee 01-20-48

If any disorder *did* occur officers were then faced with a difficulty. To make an arrest would require at least two officers to escort the arrested person away. However, this would remove officers from the scene and reduce the police's ability to control the situation and deal with any further disorder. Arrests therefore reduced the police's operational ability and could increase the chances of further disorder.

*'All we're doing when we start making arrests is playing into their* [the saboteurs] *hands because then you've got a hunt that is not policed at all.'* Interviewee 20-35-50

*'We will arrest when we can and when we think it is appropriate to do so and that is almost always determined by the numbers of officers that we've got there to be able to carry it out.'* Interviewee 01-20-48

Therefore arrests were usually made only when sufficient numbers of officers were present or a serious offence had been committed. The constraint on the making of arrests had important implications for the use of the CJPOA provisions since it meant that officers at fox hunts generally sought to keep the peace rather than enforce the law.

## Approaches to policing hunts

The unpredictability of hunts and implications for policing on the day led to three different approaches.

### Intelligence-led policing

While all officers were receptive to any intelligence which might help them, some placed a particular emphasis upon an *intelligence-led approach* to the policing of hunts. Here, intelligence was used to alert officers to whether any hunts in their area were to be the focus of saboteur activity. Information could come from inter-force liaison, ACPO's intelligence units or the Animal Rights National Index[5]. Intelligence strongly dictated police staffing levels for the hunt. In some cases, on the basis of information received, only a single officer was sent to the hunt. The CJPOA provisions were accepted by officers and used when they felt it was appropriate. This approach was described as the only effective way of managing limited resources. However, officers readily conceded that if the intelligence they received was wrong they could face some serious problems in terms of policing any resulting disorder. Despite this, officers felt that if any major saboteur activity was about to occur in their area they would hear about it since the publicity involved in an event such as a 'mass sab' would lead to the police receiving information via their intelligence links. Officers might not know the exact target, but they could at least increase policing levels and be prepared.

### Pro-active policing

The second approach involved officers being committed to policing hunts on a regular basis, rather than relying heavily on intelligence to guide staffing

---

5    Based at Scotland Yard, the Animal Rights National Index collects and distributes intelligence on extreme animal rights activists. It was set up in 1986 following a rise in activity by animal liberation groups, including raids on laboratories, hoax food threats and the sending of letter bombs.

levels. Dedicated hunt teams tended to police hunts throughout the season. Relatively large numbers of officers were deployed on a regular basis and the CJPOA's provisions were used 'quite rigidly' in an attempt to put off saboteurs attending hunts in the area.

> *'On occasions we've put out quite a large policing presence and the idea is to basically scare them off, to get them to think, "Why go where there's at least 18 policemen when we can go somewhere else and they'll only be a few?" At the end of the day we just want rid of them, we don't want them here.'* Interviewee 20-35-50

Stewards were used with police consent in a number of these hunts. As a result saboteurs were described as leaving the hunts alone because they did not like the way officers policed them. Some saboteurs still regularly attended these hunts but did so in much reduced numbers. The hunts were now less likely to be the focus of a 'hit' involving large numbers of saboteurs bent on causing disruption. Instead, saboteurs were now believed to be travelling to hunts in other forces which were 'softer targets'. When pro-active tactics were used, hunts were described as now being much more manageable, leading to a reduction in staffing levels and in the use of the CJPOA provisions.

## Agreement-led policing

The third approach to policing hunts was very different. Officers sought to make the policing of hunts more predictable and less disorderly by using a mixture of negotiation and coercion to create informal rulings and agreements between themselves, the hunt and the saboteurs. This agreement-led approach commonly focused on the activity of stewards since these people were viewed by a number of officers as instrumental in the escalation of disorder. In some cases officers were able to prevent the use of stewards by threatening to stop policing the hunt if the organisers did not agree to withdraw them. In one area officers successfully brokered an arrangement in which the hunt dispensed with stewards and, in turn, the saboteur organisers limited the number of saboteurs attending the hunt. In two other cases officers agreed with MFHs that a fox would not be dug out if it went to ground since this activity was a common flashpoint for disorder. Agreement was also reached with saboteurs not to use whips and anti-scent sprays.

> *'Because we have this working relationship with the sabs, we actually know who they are, we know the leaders and the ones to talk to. We know the ones that are influencing the other ones, so we know the ones to talk to.'* Interviewee 36-33-43

The agreement-led approach had implications for the use of the CJPOA provisions. Initially, the creation of provisions to deal with hunt saboteuring led to relations between police and saboteurs souring and a number of agreements being called off as the CJPOA passed through Parliament. However, once the provisions were available they too became a bargaining chip in negotiations with saboteurs. In two cases within different police forces officers had agreed with saboteurs not to use the CJPOA provisions relating to aggravated trespass if the saboteurs observed two rules[6]. The first of these was that the saboteurs must not act violently, wear masks or carry sticks when at the hunt. The second was that they must limit the number of saboteurs attending the hunt and not encourage other saboteur groups to target hunts in the area. Co-operation was so great with regard to the second rule that in both cases saboteur organisers would contact officers to give them prior notice of the number of saboteurs likely to be attending any future hunt.

> 'I have said to the Saboteur Association that we deal with, if you send more than is manageable for me to go up and talk to then I will simply have to implement the new powers and you will be arrested or taken off the land. But if you send me a manageable number then I will negotiate.' Interviewee 38-02-37

Such arrangements were based on local relations with saboteurs and could differ from division to division. However, there was some indication that where the agreement-led approach existed it tended to be adopted as a force-wide policy. The agreement not to use the CJPOA provisions meant that officers policed hunts using the powers available to them prior to the CJPOA, typically common law breach of the peace. However, these arrangements had led to strained relations with members of the local hunts who made their opposition to this agreement clear. Other officers who had heard of these arrangements were also critical. Some found it hard to see how hunts could be effectively policed under such agreements or how officers could possibly refuse to use provisions available to them.

> 'I cannot understand how a force cannot use the CJPOA, I depend on sections 68 and 69. I do not pick and choose what bits of legislation I use, if it is there I will use it.' Interviewee 37-12-26

> 'How do these forces face the landowners who are saying, "there is an offence happening on my land, it is disrupting my lawful activity and it's costing me £10,000 a day, why aren't you doing something about it?"' Interviewee 13-06-10

---

6    This finding is supported by news articles concerning the CJPOA and the activities of hunt saboteurs (Carty, 1996).

## Use of the CJPOA measures

Unsurprisingly, the introduction of the CJPOA provisions was generally welcomed by officers, although the strength of the welcome was related to the way in which officers approached the policing of hunts.

> '*It's the cornerstone if you like of what we do. Prior to that we had to use the old common law and the Public Order Act which really wasn't suitable. Now I have to say that I have all the powers I require.*' Interviewee 01-20-48

> '*When you are actually on the scene this kind of legislation is very useful.*' Interviewee 13-06-10

> '*I think whereas before we were airy fairy with the offence, at least aggravated trespass is a bit clearer.*' Interviewee 31-04-45

Dissenting voices came from officers who had either entered into agreements with saboteurs or those who had experienced cases failing in court. The latter complained that the new provisions were 'poorly worded' and 'difficult to enforce', or had a 'bleak future'.

It was unclear what impact the CJPOA provisions had on the level of saboteur activity. On the one hand, one officer claimed that his use of the provisions, along with his pro-active approach, had led to a reduction in the level of staff required to police a hunt. On the other hand, another officer using the same approach believed the provisions had led to hunts being more difficult to police since groups of saboteurs had stopped regularly attending specific hunts in predictable numbers and now tended to band together and arrive unexpectedly at hunts in large numbers.

The difficulties associated with the making of arrests during a hunt have already been mentioned and interviewees were keen to emphasise that the use of the CJPOA provisions depended on having enough personnel present and the discretion of each police officer.

> '*Now whether or not we're able to implement them is another matter. I mean it's about the discretion of the police officers at the scene. Because if we are outnumbered then there is absolutely no way, other than calling up for assistance, that we are physically capable of enforcing the Criminal Justice Act or indeed any other act.*' Interviewee 01-20-48

> '*The difficulty with aggravated trespass is that if we send four officers and there's 25 sabs. We say: "Right, we've seen some*

*balaclavas, we've seen some who have been intimidating and those people can be said to be committing unlawful behaviour". We arrest them which takes two officers for each person and we're left with 23 sabs and no officers. The reality is we just can't do that because then we leave the hunt with nobody there at all.'*
Interviewee 20-35-50

## The scope of aggravated trespass (s68)

A range of saboteur activities was described by officers as falling within the statutory definition of aggravated trespass. Forms of intimidation cited included the wearing of balaclavas and masks, the possession of staves and the shouting of abuse at members of the field. Obstruction and disruption could include jumping in front of horses, sitting on top of a fox's earth to prevent it being dug out, use of anti-scent spray and attempts to 'draw' the hounds.

One example of officers making arrests using s68 involved a hunt which, shortly after having started, ran a fox to ground. Having failed to flush out the fox using terriers, members of the hunt began to dig it out. The hunt had been attended by a group of eight saboteurs who, having been watching the scene from some distance, then moved towards the earth in order to prevent any further digging. The three officers present sought to stop the saboteurs making their way to the fox's earth, telling them that they were on private land which they were not allowed to enter. In response, the saboteurs stated that they were not trespassing since they were following a public footpath. This claim led to some hesitation on the officers' part and soon all eight saboteurs were sitting on top of the fox's earth, preventing any further digging and exchanging verbal abuse with members of the hunt.

The landowner was already present and informed officers that there was no footpath across the field and that he wanted the saboteurs removed. The inspector in charge then formally told the saboteurs that they were trespassing and obstructing a lawful activity, and asked them to leave. They refused and were asked several more times to leave by the inspector who then told them that they were under arrest. With three officers, two cars and eight suspects the inspector had to call for more officers and a transit van. However, since those officers who might have provided immediate support had been called to a local football match it was some time before any officers arrived. During this time the saboteurs remained on top of the fox's earth. When it became apparent that police support was about to arrive, the saboteurs attempted to escape. Three were immediately restrained by the officers and the rest were caught soon afterwards by officers arriving in support.

The above example and other interviews showed at least some officers to be unclear about what the terms 'land' and 'trespass' did and did not refer to. Some officers were not always sure whether they could use their powers on footpaths and bridleways as these may not be defined by the CJPOA as 'land'. In fact, the Act's definition of 'land', while not including highways, *does include* footpaths and bridleways. Furthermore, on a number of occasions protesters stated that they were on a public footpath or bridlepath and could not be trespassing since they had public right-of-way. However, according to case law, while a person may cross and re-cross an area by a public footpath, if that person exceeds this right and uses the path for other purposes (e.g. to protest from) they become a trespasser[7]. If, therefore, protesters sought to obstruct or disrupt a hunt from a public footpath or intimidated members of a hunt from this position, then officers would have the option of using s68. However, officers would not have the power to prevent people who might be about to engage in these activities from entering a piece of land by using a public footpath.

## Directing protesters to leave land (s69)

The practice of directing people to leave land was described by some officers as a way of limiting trouble and 'preventing situations getting out of hand'[8]. A number of senior officers relied on a laminated card when reading out the direction to ensure they used the right wording since some saboteurs were known to record the making of directions in case they were made incorrectly. Saboteurs generally complied with directions to leave land. However, two issues arose from the use of s69.

The first issue centred on who was the 'senior officer present at the scene' for the purposes of the legislation. This arose in two court cases described by officers. The first concerned what was likely to have been the first use by the police of the CJPOA public order measures and occurred at a hunt in the middle of November 1994. The court proceedings gave an estimate of the number of protesters and saboteurs attending the hunt as between 200 and 400. These people successfully managed to disrupt the hunt, to the extent that it was prematurely ended. Twenty four people subsequently appeared in court, with the majority being accused of offences under s68 or s69. The subsequent trial led to eight people being convicted for aggravated trespass and one for obstructing a police officer. However, six people accused of failing to leave land when directed had their cases dismissed. In court it had been argued by the prosecution that the officer giving the saboteurs this

---

7. Here the case most often mentioned is from the nineteenth century and involved a man called Harrison who was deemed to have been a trespasser on land when disrupting the Duke of Rutland's shoot from a public footpath (*Harrison* v *Duke of Rutland* [1893] 1 QB 142.

8. One officer stated that: '...s69 is really there for two situations. Firstly, before there's any major confrontation you use it to get rid of them off the land. Secondly, major trouble has taken place and you get lots of stragglers who are part of the main bunch, who might regroup and cause further trouble – s69 is useful for them as well.' Interviewee 01-20-48

direction, although only a police constable, was the most senior officer present. After some debate the magistrate disagreed with this point of view and stated that the senior officer was the person in charge of the operation, who happened to be some distance away. Since the original direction to leave land was invalid so too were the subsequent arrests.

The second court case again involved a police constable who had given a direction to leave land. In court no objection was made to this direction coming from a low-ranking officer at the scene rather than the officer in charge of the operation. Instead, the argument centred on whether another police constable also at the scene should have given the direction, because of his greater seniority. Since both officers were of the same rank, seniority centred on age and length of service. The magistrate ruled that seniority was based on the latter. So although the direction had been made by the older officer, because he had four months less service in the police than the other officer present the direction was invalid and the case was dismissed.

A second issue concerned the situation where someone returned to the land having been directed from it. As found in relation to other powers, officers stated that it was common for those who complied with the direction not to have their personal details taken, thereby making it difficult to establish that they had in fact returned to land. When policing a hunt, any attempt to record people's identity was made difficult by the saboteurs' practice of wearing balaclavas and sometimes changing clothes. Officers were also concerned about what amounted to a return to the land. Did it mean the same spot, the same field or a wider area? Should a person directed to leave the land who then appears in another field sometime later, be arrested or again directed to leave land? In addition, any direction which made returning to land an offence during the next three months was of limited use towards the end of the hunt season since much of this ban would fall outside the time period when other events occurred.

Only one example in the research was found of saboteurs being arrested for returning to land. This was another case in which a hunt had run a fox to ground in a copse and was seeking to dig it out. Saboteurs attempted to stop this activity but, having been directed away, were arrested when they returned after a short while. Despite this example, it was more common for officers simply to give saboteurs another direction to leave.

*'The problem is that they're wearing balaclavas and when you remove them from the area you've got no power to take their names and addresses so how do you know if they came back within three months? You don't! It's a simple answer. So we settle for the fact that we're just removing them from land.'* Interviewee 36-33-43

## Evidential issues

A central theme emerging from the interviews was the difficulty of prosecuting people allegedly committing offences at hunts. Those defendants appeared ready to contest prosecutions on issues such as whether the proper regulations had been followed while they were in custody and whether the landowner had given permission for hunting on his or her land. The difficulty of contacting landowners who had been called to testify on the latter point and the unwillingness of magistrates to accept a land agent instead had led to a number of cases being dismissed. Officers also described the problems of establishing what had happened when they arrived at a scene following serious disorder, with conflicting accounts from both sides making the chances of any prosecution very low. Even when officers stayed close to the hunt or the saboteurs, it could still be difficult to establish after the event that someone had crossed the line from lawful protest and become involved in illegal actions. Common defences provided by saboteurs included that they did not receive or hear a direction to leave land or that they were lost or seeking a footpath, rather than intending to obstruct or disrupt the hunt.

> *'I think there's quite a lot of saboteurs been taken to court and we've lost because they've argued that they weren't doing anything and we've not really had brilliant evidence so they've been found not guilty.'* Interviewee 31-04-45

In response to this problem officers tended to take video equipment with them when a large number of saboteurs were expected at a hunt, enabling incidents of violence and disorder to be recorded along with those participating[9]. Videoing was also useful to collect evidence on the appearance of saboteurs, although opinions differed on how effective this might be in court[10]. Officers were not always able to video incidents and at other times the quality of the recording could be poor. However, video recording had enabled a number of evidential issues to be clarified with the Crown Prosecution Service (CPS) and had been of assistance in securing prosecutions and convictions in some cases.

Relations with the CPS were another issue raised by officers. A great deal of frustration was expressed at the level of evidence apparently required in order for a prosecution to go ahead. In some cases CPS staff had attended hunts with officers in order to clarify issues surrounding lawful protest and the evidential requirements for offences such as aggravated trespass. However, in other cases CPS staff were criticised for not taking the offences

---

9   Another response by officers was to make sure that they had detailed maps to hand in order to record for any further proceedings the exact route of the hunt, nearby public footpaths and the location of any disorder.

10   Despite the practice of swapping clothes, some officers stated that saboteurs could be consistently identified by recording their footwear which was rarely changed. In response one officer stated he would be interested to see if someone could be convicted on 'the strength of a pair of Nike trainers'.

seriously enough, letting their emotions get in the way and having some sympathy for the hunt saboteurs. Both the discontinuing of cases by the CPS and the dismissal of cases by the courts were described as affecting officers' confidence when policing hunts.

> *'It causes me problems because it has a knock-on effect. It plants in the mind of the saboteurs that they can get away with it, that the law is in disrepute, and it demoralises my officers.'* Interviewee 37-12-26

> *'Because of this past history of people getting away with it, that's another reason why officers are loathe to jump in.'* Interviewee 31-04-45

## Part two: environmental protest

In addition to fox hunting and other field sports, the measures relating to aggravated trespass have been applied to environmental protest. The following section describes how the provisions were used during the early development of the Newbury bypass (probably the most high-profile of environmental protests since the introduction of the CJPOA), and during two one-day protests over nuclear power and the development of a quarry.

## The Newbury bypass

After many years of argument approval for the development of a bypass at Newbury, Berkshire was given in July 1995. Following opposition to the building of roads at Twyford Down and in Wanstead, East London, the Newbury bypass became a focus for environmental groups protesting about the government's roads building programme. When contractors began clearing the route of the bypass in early January 1996 they were met by a wide range of well-organised protest groups seeking to hinder or stop the building of the road through peaceful protest, legal contestation and direct action[11]. In particular, a large number of protesters were living along the ten-mile route of the bypass in nine camps with names such as Tree Pixie Village and Granny Ash. The main task of contractors seeking to clear the site was the felling and removal of the large number of trees along the planned route. In response, protesters had built an estimated 60 treehouses, 30–40 feet above the ground, stocked with water and food, and linked to each other by ropeways. Several tunnels, apparently unable to bear the weight of heavy vehicles, had also been built and made ready for habitation. Furthermore, so as to obstruct the contractors, protesters had made preparations to padlock

---

11   The clearing of trees and most of the protesters living on the bypass route took three months and ended in early April 1996.

themselves to trees and machinery, and chain themselves to concrete-filled barrels set in the ground.

In order to understand the use of the CJPOA provisions at Newbury, it is relevant to provide some background information about those groups, other than the protesters, who were present during the clearing of the route. The development of the bypass was carried out by the *Highways Agency* (part of the Department of Transport) which, in order to help clear the site, employed several hundred *security guards* from a private security company[12]. Approximately 600 guards were employed to work on the bypass when clearance of the route first began. As unskilled, casual labour, their main task was to act as a cordon, literally standing shoulder to shoulder around a specific area where clearance work was being conducted and thereby preventing any protesters gaining access[13]. In order to remove those protesters living on the route of the bypass the Highways Agency used the civil law to apply for possession orders from the High Court. Although challenged by anti-bypass campaigners, these applications were granted. The evictions then became the responsibility of the *Under-Sheriff of Berkshire*[14]. The Under-Sheriff carried out evictions with the help of bailiffs and specialist 'rope access' firms employed to remove protesters from trees. Finally, the safety of those on the route of the bypass was the responsibility of another government organisation, the Health and Safety Executive (HSE). Members of the HSE were present as the route was cleared and the protesters removed. The extent to which the constructors complied with the regulations was raised later in court by protesters.

## The police role

Because the route of the bypass crossed two police force areas, the associated policing was a joint exercise between Thames Valley and Hampshire Constabularies. The so-called 'Operation Prospect' involved around 150 officers at its height[15]. As in the policing of fox hunts, officers described their main role as refereeing between the two sides, therefore ensuring that protesters were able to demonstrate peacefully and that contractors were able to carry out their work.

*I'm not personally concerned with whether the road gets built or not, but what I am concerned with is the rule of law and the rule of law will prevail and be maintained, so that if I see a contractor or a security officer doing something that is unlawful they will be*

---

12  Security guards were also employed to deal with another case of roads protest included in the research. This involved the development of the A299 or 'Thanet Way' in Kent.

13  The Highways Agency also employed a Southampton-based private detective agency to provide surveillance and information-gathering services.

14  The initial evictions were contested in the High Court on the grounds that the compulsory purchase orders for the land were invalid and an environmental impact assessment was required under European law.

15  It was agreed that Thames Valley would provide two-thirds of the officers required and Hampshire one-third.

*dealt with in exactly the same way as a protester, and that's the line you try to take.'* Interviewee 38-48-04

However, officers took a less detached position when protesters were being evicted, since they tended to accompany the Under-Sheriff and the bailiffs to ensure the possession orders were enforced and that the Under-Sheriff 'got his job done'.

## Use of the CJPOA provisions

The conflict surrounding the building of the Newbury bypass led to the greatest use up to that date of the public order provisions contained in the CJPOA. During what some protesters called the 'Third Battle of Newbury', 988 arrests were made, including 356 people for aggravated trespass. The vast majority of these occurred in the first three months, while the route was being cleared of trees and protesters. Of those arrested, 59 were cautioned and 258 prosecuted. Aggravated trespass, together with 'the obstruction of a court officer' (linked to evictions by the Under-Sheriff) were the most common charges brought by the police.

Arrests for aggravated trespass were described as usually occurring when protesters breached a cordon of security guards and climbed trees or chained themselves to machinery. Such activities were taken to amount to obstruction or disruption, within the meaning of the legislation. However there were also some instances too of intimidation, which led to arrests under s68. One concerned the driver of a lorry who had been employed to remove a waste skip from the site of some recent evictions. On arrival the vehicle was surrounded by a group of protesters who recorded the company's name and telephone number, and allegedly made a series of threats to the driver. Complaining that the telephone number was also his home number and concerned about the repercussions if he actually removed the skip, the driver refused to carry out this task and left the site[16].

The large number of arrests for aggravated trespass at the bypass may, to some extent, reflect the real level of conflict surrounding the clearing of the site. However, compared with the relatively low-level policing of fox hunting, it may also reflect the large number of officers present at Newbury to deal with disorder. Clearly, a degree of conflict was almost inevitably going to occur during the clearing of the bypass route, and this was likely to happen on a daily basis and in specific areas (those where clearance work was taking place). This predictability meant that a broadly sufficient number of officers could be deployed at the right places and times to deal with

---

16. Early in the clearance of the bypass, a Reading coach company contracted to transport security guards to work was targeted by protesters who, early one morning, had chained themselves to vehicles and buildings at its base, resulting in severe disruption. Other companies allegedly received threats or were bombarded by faxes

disorder. Because of their numbers they were able to make arrests and process the prisoners involved without significantly detracting from their ability to deal with further disorder. The CJPOA also gave the police the power to place conditions on bail after someone has been charged. At Newbury this power was used heavily in conjunction with aggravated trespass charges[17]. Much to the irritation of campaigners the police thereby sought to limit any future disorder by stipulating that those charged with offences were not to return to the site of the bypass or were to report to a particular police station every day (see Vidal,1996).

Unsurprisingly considering the frequency with which they were used, officers had positive views on the utility of the aggravated trespass provisions. At road demonstrations prior to the CJPOA such as Twyford Down, the police had tended to make arrests for common law breach of the peace. However, this was seen as inappropriate for the kind of behaviour involved and highly restrictive in terms of sentencing options since the outcome was invariably a bind-over. The new measures were viewed as closely fitting the actions of protesters and carrying a greater sanction in the event of conviction.

While aggravated trespass was used extensively at Newbury, the related power to direct people from land (s69) was rarely applied. During the first seven months of Operation Prospect only seven out of 866 charges were for s69 offences (failure to comply with a direction to leave land). The low use of this power arose because many of the protesters were actually resident upon the land from which they were likely to be directed. The legality of directing someone away from the place where they were resident, even though they may be squatting, was open to question. More importantly, the use of s69 to direct protesters from their self-made shelters, known as 'benders', was thrown into question by another piece of legislation which forbids the use of excessive force to remove people from 'premises'[18]. Having sought legal advice from a police force solicitor, officers in charge of the operation decided against challenging this argument in court. A decision was therefore made not to apply s69 to those living on the bypass route and instead to leave their removal to the Highways Agency, High Court writs, and the Under-Sheriff.

As well as making arrests for acts of violence and criminal damage, the police exercised their powers to deal with offences related to the highway. Since aggravated trespass could only be committed on 'land', officers used various Acts to deal with direct action by protesters, aimed at vehicles and staff travelling to work on the construction of the bypass. In a number of cases powers designed to deal with picketing in industrial disputes were used in instances where protesters sought to prevent 'lawful activity' by

---

17  Figures for the first two months of Operation Prospect show that around three-quarters of those charged with aggravated trespass had conditions placed on their bail.

18  Section 6 of the Criminal Law Act 1977 provides protection to squatters by prohibiting any person from using or threatening unlawful violence for the purpose of securing entry into any premises.

intimidation or by obstructing lorries, other heavy plant, and coaches carrying security guards. No arrests were made for breach of the peace which, as already noted, was often used in similar circumstances prior to the introduction of the aggravated trespass provisions.

## Prosecutions for aggravated trespass

A central issue in prosecutions for aggravated trespass was whether the activity which was the focus of protesters' action was in fact 'lawful'. Defence lawyers argued that failure to comply with health and safety legislation could render the road contractors' activities unlawful. Legal arguments therefore focused on such issues as whether work areas were effectively cordoned off, the extent of the 'clear area' around a chain saw, and whether a chain saw was turned off as soon as a cordon was breached. Magistrates tended to refuse invitations from either prosecution or defence to provide general rulings concerning safety matters and instead treated each case separately. Officers had hoped that some general rulings would be made since they believed many protesters were likely to contest each case and call a large number of witnesses in an attempt to obstruct the local court system and increase the costs associated with the bypass. While prosecutions may have been contested, the chances of a successful defence appeared small. Of the 217 prosecutions for aggravated trespass resulting from Operation Prospect, 180 produced a guilty verdict (a conviction rate of 83%)[19]. However, around three-quarters of those convicted received conditional discharges, ranging from six months to two years.

## Other cases of environmental protest

The research also examined two other cases of environmental protest which differed from the long period of activity at Newbury. They both involved examples of well-organised and non-violent direct action lasting only a few hours. The first case involved a demonstration on Easter Monday, April 1995, organised by Greenpeace at the British Nuclear Fuels (BNFL) site at Sellafield in Cumbria. Up to 250 protesters entered the site at various points and attempted to interrupt work taking place there. Various areas on the site were targeted. For example, some protesters chained themselves to the inside and outside of a large container deposited at the site's main entrance, effectively blocking access. The protesters successfully reached and entered the site without any prior warning reaching BNFL Officers from the local constabulary and the Atomic Energy Authority Constabulary were then called to the scene and either began making arrests or removed people from the site without using s69.

---

19   Thirty four appeals resulted from these convictions, all of which were disallowed or abandoned

During the protest ten people shackled themselves to a railway line known as 'Street 12'. This led to a train carrying an empty nuclear fuel flask being unable to travel from one part of the Sellafield site to another. These protesters were originally arrested under s5 of the Public Order Act 1986, but were subsequently charged with and prosecuted for aggravated trespass. As at Newbury, the defence contested the case by questioning the lawfulness of the activity taking place on the site. The specific focus was on BNFL's compliance with safety procedures, as outlined in the company's 'site licence' and other related documents. The case was hampered by the majority of documentary evidence arriving only on the first day of the trial, with other important paperwork only being produced immediately prior to witnesses giving related evidence. BNFL was allegedly reticent about disclosing the required evidence because it believed Greenpeace was using the trial as an information-gathering exercise on the working practices of the company.

After much argument in court, the case hinged on documents which dictated how the nuclear fuel flask should be handled and the records that should be made. The magistrate stated that 'serious errors' had been made in the completion of this documentation, 'which must be attributed to more than mere negligence'. The implication of these errors was that the Crown could not prove beyond reasonable doubt that the movement of the nucleur fuel flask was a lawful activity. The case was therefore dismissed. The prosecution also failed due to the wording of the charge which stated that BNFL 'was about to engage in' lawful activity and that the defendants 'intended to have the effect of *disrupting* that activity'. In his summing up the magistrate stated that the protesters' presence on the rail track meant that the movement of the train and fuel flask never began; legally therefore, the movement of the flask was 'obstructed' not 'disrupted' since no activity had begun.

The second case of environmental protest centred on Whatley Quarry in Somerset, which, as one of the largest limestone quarries in Europe, provides aggregates for road-building. The quarry and its private owners were the focus of a protest by Earth First!, who sought to highlight the environmental damage caused by a proposed extension to the site which would considerably increase its size. Unlike the Greenpeace protest at Sellafield, Avon and Somerset Constabulary and the quarry's owners were forewarned about this event via publicity on the internet and were therefore able to make preparations. Concerned that arrests under aggravated trespass could not be made if the owners stopped work at the quarry prior to the protest, officers advised the company to keep at least some work going at the site. Furthermore, because the police felt that security at the quarry was not their responsibility, the owners employed around 70 private security guards who were responsible for vulnerable areas on the site, such as the main gate and the offices. Between 80 and 300 protesters entered the quarry and caused damage to equipment and loss of business estimated at between £125,000 and £300,000.

Although ready to deal with the protest, officers did not arrive at the quarry until after the private security guards could no longer deal with the protesters and work had to be stopped. On the police's arrival, a s69 direction to leave was given via a megaphone, which apparently had little impact on the protesters. Officers then began to make arrests for aggravated trespass and failure to comply with the direction. Around 150 officers were involved in policing the protest and a large number of arrests were initially made. These led to a significant proportion of officers being drawn away from the quarry and in order to maintain an effective police presence a decision was made that no more arrests were to be made except for serious offences such as physical violence or substantial criminal damage. By this stage officers stated that the protest was dying down. A total of 58 protesters were arrested, of whom 55 were charged. At court a number of defendants unsuccessfully contested their cases, stating that their trespass was not aggravated since they did nothing actively to disrupt quarrying. However, the magistrate accepted the prosecution's argument that their mere presence compromised safety and disrupted normal activity. Other defendants argued that they were making genuine attempts to comply with police instructions to leave the site at the time of arrest, leading to acquittal in five cases.

## Use of provisions, and number of cautions and prosecutions

Police figures show that 122 people were arrested for aggravated trespass across eight forces during 1995 and that directions to leave land were given on 17 occasions across five forces. Court statistics for England and Wales show that 359 people were prosecuted for aggravated trespass in 1996, compared with 111 in 1995 (see Table 4.1). This threefold increase in prosecutions during 1996 was directly the result of the large number of arrests made at the Newbury bypass protest.

Just over half those prosecuted for the offence of aggravated trespass were convicted (1995: 58%; 1996: 59%). This figure is lower than the overall conviction rate for magistrates' courts, where around 80 per cent of cases result in conviction (Home Office, 1997). Since the conviction rate for cases at the Newbury bypass was over 80 per cent, the low conviction rate for agggravated trespass is likely to be due to other environmental protesters and animal rights activists successfully contesting their cases. Compared with aggravated trespass, there were relatively few prosecutions for failure to leave land. Of the 211 people convicted of aggravated trespass in 1996, 111 were given conditional discharges, 93 were given fines averaging £114 and one was given a probation order. Only four people (2% of those convicted) received prison sentences. These ranged from four to six weeks. All four had been arrested for offences at the Newbury bypass. Of the four people convicted of failing to leave land under s69, three were given fines averaging £87 and one was given a community sentence order.

### Table 4.1: Cautions and court proceedings for aggravated trespass (s68) and failure to leave land when directed (s69)

| | | Cautions | Prosecutions | Convictions |
|---|---|---|---|---|
| Aggravated trespass (s68) | 1995 | 7 | 111 | 64 |
| | 1996 | 14 | 359 | 211 |
| Failure to leave land (s69) | 1995 | 11 | 15 | 12 |
| | 1996 | 0 | 27 | 4 |

## Key points

### *Fox hunting*

- In order to overcome difficulties associated with hunts, officers had tended to adopt one of three approaches. The 'intelligence-led' and 'pro-active' approaches both made use of the CJPOA measures. The 'agreement-led' approach involved officers, as part of wider negotiations, agreeing not to use the CJPOA measures in return for specific concessions from saboteurs.

- The introduction of the CJPOA measures was generally welcomed by officers. However, interviewees emphasised that their use depended on the amount of personnel at the scene and the discretion of each police officer.

- Activities interpreted by officers as constituting aggravated trespass by saboteurs included: the wearing of balaclavas and masks; possession of staves; shouting abuse at members of the hunt; jumping in front of horses; obstructing the digging of a fox from its earth; the use of anti-scent spray; and attempts to 'draw' the hounds.

- Saboteurs and protesters generally complied with directions made by officers under s69 to leave land. However, arguments about whether the person making the direction was the 'senior officer at the scene' led to a number of prosecutions being dismissed at court.

- It was rare for people to be arrested for returning to land after having been directed from it (s69). This was because those who complied with police orders and left the land rarely had their personal details taken, thereby making it difficult to establish conclusively that they had in fact returned. Officers were also concerned about whether returning to land meant a return to the same spot, same field or a wider area.

- Providing enough evidence for a successful prosecution was said to be difficult, although the use of video equipment had been found to be useful. Discontinuance by the CPS and the failure of a number of cases in court had led to frustration among officers, with some complaining that this was having an impact on the policing of hunts.

## Environmental protest

- The police operation relating to the building of the Newbury bypass involved the greatest single use of the public order measures contained in the CJPOA. During the police operation, 356 arrests were made for aggravated trespass. Of those arrested, 258 were prosecuted.

- Arrests at Newbury for aggravated trespass were typically made when protesters allegedly breached security cordons and climbed trees, chained themselves to machinery and intimidated contractors on the site.

- The large number of arrests for aggravated trespass at Newbury may partly reflect the level of conflict on the site, but it may also reflect the nature and scale of the police response. Unlike with fox hunting, the police at Newbury were aware when disorder was going to occur and where this was likely to happen. Sufficient officers were therefore deployed at the right times and places to deal with disorder and were able to utilise the available provisions.

- The ability to make arrests for aggravated trespass was viewed as a positive development by officers, who felt that the use of breach of the peace at previous road protests was inappropriate for the behaviour in question and of limited value in terms of the sanctions involved.

- The power to direct people from land (s69) was rarely used at Newbury. This was mainly because other legislation appeared to offer some protection to those living on the site and threw into question the use of s69.

- At Newbury and in other instances of environmental protest, prosecutions for aggravated trespass tended to be challenged at court on the grounds that the work being obstructed or disrupted was unlawful. Challenges might focus on health and safety procedures or on other related regulations.

- Police figures show that 122 people were arrested for aggravated trespass during 1995 and that directions to leave land were given on 17 occasions. Court statistics for England and Wales show that 359 people were prosecuted for aggravated trespass in 1996, compared with 111 in 1995. Just over half those prosecuted for aggravated trespass were convicted.

# 5 Conclusion

This report has examined the use of the public order provisions contained in the CJPOA 1994. In this final chapter the main findings of the research are discussed.

## The effectiveness of directions

The CJPOA public order provisions contain three possible responses to nuisance or disorder on land. The first involves the use of directions to remove people from a particular site or to prevent them travelling to a particular location. The second involves the seizure of vehicles and sound equipment. The third involves the power of arrest for a series of offences resulting from the non-compliance with directions, or behaviour defined as 'aggravated trespass'. It is clear from this research that the principal activity carried out under the CJPOA public order provisions was the use of directions. Furthermore, people were generally found to comply when directions were issued, and any disorder usually being resolved. For example, officers dealing with raves typically directed people away from the site using s63, and directed others not to proceed towards the event using s65. Compliance with these directions meant that the site could be cleared and the event successfully dealt with without any arrests being made.

The successful application of directions meant that there were relatively few prosecutions. While directions in response to trespass on land (s61) were given a total of 67 times during 1995, in the same year only nine people were either cautioned or prosecuted for offences under this section. The picture was the same for the rave provisions. During 1995 directions to leave a rave (s63) were used nine times and directions not to proceed to a rave (s65) 32 times. However, no cautions or prosecutions resulted from the use of these provisions. The greatest number of prosecutions resulted from directions to leave land under s69 during 1995, when it was used 17 times and led to 11 cautions and 15 prosecutions.

## Prosecutions under the CJPOA provisions

The greatest number of prosecutions resulted not from non-compliance with directions but from the offence of aggravated trespass (s68). A total of 122 arrests were made during 1995 in relation to protests about blood sports or the environment, with these leading to 111 prosecutions and seven cautions. Unlike trespass on land, cautioning was relatively rare for aggravated trespass. Significantly, just over one-half of those prosecuted for aggravated trespass in both 1995 and 1996 were convicted. This proportion is relatively low for magistrates' courts in which around 80 per cent of cases resulted in a conviction, and reflects the extent to which well-organised groups of defendants contested their cases on the basis that the provisions had been incorrectly used.

Those convicted under any of the CJPOA provisions were most likely to be given a conditional discharge or a fine. Probation and community service orders were rare, as were custodial sentences. Only four out of the 298 people convicted under the provisions during 1995 and 1996 served a prison term, all four having been convicted of aggravated trespass at the Newbury bypass.

## Variations in the use of the CJPOA provisions

The research found three main variations in the use of the CJPOA provisions. Firstly, although it is as yet too early to identify longer-term trends, it appears that the amount to which the provisions have been used has varied considerably over time. For example, a threefold rise occurred in prosecutions for aggravated trespass between 1995 and 1996. This rise was due to the protests at Newbury bypass and the resulting police operation. In general police operations, long-term protests and other activities involving potential disorder were found to have had a strong impact on the use of the powers from year to year.

Secondly, the extent to which forces had made use of the CJPOA provisions varied, with 22 of the 43 forces in England and Wales applying the provisions during 1995. Furthermore, of those forces using the provisions some had drawn on them more heavily than others. For example, one force exercised s61 16 times in one year, while most used it only once or twice. Such variations may partly reflect that the pattern of public disorder is not random. In particular, forces with a large number of gypsies, New Age Travellers, hunts or a controversial road development within their boundaries may be more likely to use the provisions than others. However, the variations may also reflect differing police practices and levels of willingness to use the provisions, discussed in the next section.

Thirdly, the research also found that the situations in which the provisions were used varied widely in terms of their size, seriousness and duration. For example, the circumstances in which officers used s69 to direct people from land ranged from a minor instance of disorder at a fox hunt involving one or two people to a serious disturbance at a quarry involving several hundred protesters.

## Police practices and public order policing

The application of the CJPOA provisions on particular occasions tended to depend on three factors relating to the practicalities and constraints of public order policing. The first of these concerned officers' skills in managing public order situations and keeping the peace. Here the CJPOA provisions were viewed by officers as one of a number of resources available to them when engaged in public order encounters, and not necessarily to be drawn upon as their first response. On some occasions officers could skilfully resolve situations by drawing upon the authority of their office, their inter-personal skills and their experience of policing similar encounters in the past. As with the power of arrest, the CJPOA provisions may not be exercised during these occasions, but the explicit or tacit threat of their use could be effectively employed by officers[1]. On other occasions circumstances meant that the provisions were fully exercised. As stated above, the giving of directions was the principal activity under the CJPOA provisions. The high level of compliance and low number of arrests among the large number of people facing such directions is also partly explained by officers' abilities to manage these encounters. Giving a group of people a direction to leave a piece of land or not to proceed to a rave did not mean that they would automatically follow this command. The successful application of these directions depended on officers again drawing upon their authority and experience, and using the possibility of arrest to enforce their instructions. Officers' public order expertise, therefore was not used simply to support the CJPOA provisions, it was an integral part of their application.

The second and third factors influencing the application of the CJPOA provisions are closely linked and concern whether the police had prior warning of potential disorder and whether they deployed sufficient numbers of officers in good time. Whether sufficient officers were at the right place at the right time was particularly influential with regard to raves, fox hunting and environmental protest. How these factors combined could lead to similar forms of disorder being policed in different ways and the following examples illustrate this point.

---

1    For a discussion of the management of police-public encounters and the part played by police powers see Bittner, 1970; Chatterton, 1976; Reiner, 1992.

On a number of occasions officers described arriving at a location to find a rave in full progress and large numbers of people present. Here, even with large numbers of officers available, it was unlikely that the CJPOA provisions would have been used successfully to restore public order or to seize sound equipment. To apply the provisions to a large gathering and then seek to enforce them risked increasing disorder, possibly resulting in injuries to officers and to those attending the event. Under these circumstances few officers would seek to use the provisions to break up the rave. Instead, they sought to stop the event growing any larger and to limit the level of disorder by preventing anyone else from attending. However, at other times the police were informed of a rave prior to it commencing. In one particular example officers were made aware of a planned rave by local inhabitants early during the evening on which it was due to be held. As a result a small number of officers arrived at the site before the sound equipment had been fully set up and before many people had arrived. These officers used the provisions to direct the organisers and equipment from the site under s63, thereby effectively preventing the event from taking place.

In the instance of fox hunting, officers responsible for policing hunts found it difficult to predict when and where public order flashpoints might occur. This, together with the geographical remoteness and inaccessibility of much hunting country, meant that they were forced to police these events in the knowledge that the officers present on the day would have to deal with any disorder by themselves since any support was unlikely to arrive in time. These difficulties did not mean that the CJPOA provisions were not used, but they did lead to them being utilised in various ways. In some cases staffing levels were expanded and the relevant CJPOA provisions were used quite extensively. In other cases officers used the provisions as a bargaining chip to make informal pacts with hunt saboteurs, whereby they agreed not to apply the provisions in return for a number of concessions.

When disorder did occur at fox hunts, and at a number of environmental protests, officers were faced with a dilemma which affected the use of the CJPOA provisions. To make arrests for aggravated trespass might end any immediate disorder, but it would also draw officers away from the scene and therefore reduce the police's ability to deal effectively with any further trouble. Under such circumstances officers generally decided against using the provisions and, unless serious offences were committed, sought to separate antagonists and generally to deal with any disorder without making arrests.

In contrast to the policing of fox hunts, the cases of environmental protest at Whatley Quarry and on the site of the Newbury bypass involved enough prior warning to allow the police to deploy sufficient officers in time. At Newbury in particular it became clear that a considerable amount of protest would occur when developers began clearing the route of the bypass and that the protest was likely to occur over a long period of time and be mainly focused at specific sites. The arrests made at Newbury may reflect the number of officers deployed as much as the real level of disorder. The availability of manpower allowed arrests to be made and prisoners to be processed without significantly affecting the police's ability to deal with further disorder.

With regard to trespass on land, the CJPOA provisions appeared to have had little affect on the police's pre-existing approaches to cases of mass trespass, such as that at Castlemorton. As with large raves in progress, the chances of successfully applying the provisions and enforcing the law without serious disorder and injuries were likely to be slight. In cases involving much smaller examples of trespass, the use of the CJPOA provisions was less dependent on the deployment of sufficient officers at a particular time and place. However, other factors were influential, most notably the type of group involved in the trespass. While the provisions were found to have been used in relation to both New Age Travellers and gypsies, the willingness to direct gypsies from land using the CJPOA tended to vary from one police force to another. Use of the provisions could also vary according to relations between the police and the local authourity concerning responsibility for particular trespass sites, and the extent to which local forces were prepared to commit time and resources to this area.

The direction to leave land (s61) was found to be the most commonly used of the directions provided by the CJPOA. However, giving a direction, along with a deadline by which trespassers should have left, was not always effective in itself and those on the site commonly ignored it. Despite this, officers always enforced a direction to leave land, usually by arriving in large numbers at the site or by towing a number of vehicles onto the road in the hope that the others on the site would go of their own volition. Officers' commitment to enforcing s61 was strongly influenced by the disadvantages of the alternative option of seizing vehicles under s62. This was an extremely rare event due to the organisational problems involved, such as hiring towing lorries, removing vehicles from the site, finding storage space and addressing the issue of accommodation for those living in the vehicles. There was also the likelihood of disorder when officers sought to seize vehicles from those encamped on the site.

## Application, coherence and impact

The use of the CJPOA provisions was also related to their ease of application. This has already been touched upon in relation to the seizure of vehicles. However, it was also relevant to the powers officers have to direct people from land (ss61, 63 and 69). Under these powers it is an offence to return to the site in question within a specified time limit, yet arrests for such offences were very rare for a number of reasons. Firstly, if a person complied with the initial police direction it was unlikely that their personal details would be taken, thereby making any alleged return to land difficult to prove. Secondly, obtaining an accurate record of the identities of those directed from land was not always easy. For example, saboteurs regularly wore balaclavas and sometimes exchanged clothes; and vehicles that had been removed from a site might return having been sold to other New Age Travellers and gypsies. In the light of these difficulties, officers were likely to give another direction to leave to those they suspected of returning to a site within the specified time limit, rather than seek to activate the existing ban.

The research revealed some misunderstandings of the provisions concerning raves. Thus, some officers did not realise that the power to instruct people not to proceed towards a rave (s65) could only be used once people at the site of the rave had been directed to leave (s63). In addition, uncertainty was revealed about the relationship of the CJPOA provisions with other legislation and rulings. In particular, there was uncertainty among officers at Newbury about the relationship between the power to direct people from land (s69) and those sections of the Criminal Law Act 1997 providing protection to squatters. There was also some uncertainty about the implications for the police of the *Wealden Judgement* concerning local authority welfare responsibilities for those illegally encamped on land. Although only mentioned by a few officers, the judgement does, according to some legal commentators, extend to the police. If so, the impact on the police's ability under s61 to direct people from a site could be significant. So far this issue has not arisen in cases involving the police. There are some grounds for believing that the obligation on the police to take care of trespassers' welfare needs is not as great as that falling upon local authorities. The circumstances of each case would appear to define whether and to what extent officers should make enquiries about the personal circumstances of trespassers. When serious disorder is actually occurring, no enquiry may be necessary. However, if time allows it would be reasonable for some enquiry to be made into the welfare of the trespassers before a direction is made.

How might the impact of the CJPOA public order provisions be best summarised? Officers with experience of using the provisions were generally positive, seeing them as allowing the police to deal with disorder in a more effective manner and involving more appropriate punishments for those convicted under the related offences. However, their impact should be viewed in the light of the provisions available to the police prior to the CJPOA. In the kinds of situations covered by the research, police officers would have been in attendance irrespective of whether the CJPOA provisions were in existence or not. Therefore the Act, did not make any difference to the types of public order situation with which the police sought to deal. Prior to the CJPOA, officers had tackled these situations with recourse to existing powers and offences, such as those contained in the Public Order Act 1986, common law breach of the peace, public nuisance and criminal damage. On a number of occasions officers expressed doubt about how appropriate some of these provisions had been for the circumstances. On other occasions, when no law or powers clearly related to a situation, officers relied on their general authority, seeking to resolve the incident through a mixture of negotiation and persuasion. Contrary to what is sometimes thought, the CJPOA does not appear to have brought a wider range of public disorder within the ambit of policing. Nor does the CJPOA appear to have led to a significant change in the police's preparedness to take action in these public order situations. However, it has resulted in officers being placed in a *stronger legal position* when dealing with these incidents.

# Appendix A: The legal definition of a gypsy

Legally the term 'gypsy' has been interpreted in a number of ways (for a full discussion see Geary and O'Shea, 1995). While race relations legislation has tended to define gypsies as an ethnic group, legislation dealing with caravan sites has focused upon a non-ethnic nomadic definition. In the spirit of the latter legislation, s24 of the Caravan Sites and Control of Development Act 1960, as amended by s80 of the CJPOA, defines 'gypsies' as:

> *'...persons of a nomadic habit of life whatever their race or origin, but* [not including] *members of an organised group of travelling showmen, or persons engaged in travelling circuses, travelling together as such'.*

In *R* v *South Hams District Council, ex parte Gibb* (1994) *The Times*, 8 June, CA, the Court of Appeal upheld this definition, while adding the requirement that there should be some connection between the wandering or travelling of those concerned and the means whereby they made their livelihood. Whether New Age Travellers can be viewed as gypsies centres on whether their movement from place to place is connected to their means of livelihood or not. Case law suggests that this may be so, with some travellers arguing that their movement is linked to local arts and of crafts markets, casual agricultural employment and temporary factory work (see *R* v *Gloucester CC, ex parte Dutton* (1991) 24 HLR 246, at 248–205). However, the repeal of the obligation on local authorities to provide sites for gypsies means there is little reason for travellers to claim the status of gypsies. This label now only holds significant benefit in the area of planning and not in the area of securing a public site and resisting eviction proceedings (see Clements and Low-Beer, 1996).

# References

**Association of Chief Police Officers.** (1996). *Guidance Document: Criminal Justice and Public Order Act 1994.* (unpublished).

**Baxter, J.** (1992). 'Castlemorton and Beyond'. *Policing*, Vol 8, No.3, Autumn, p222-231.

**Bittner, E.** (1970). *The Functions of the Police in a Modern Society.* Maryland: NIMH

**Card, R. and Ward, R.** (1994). *The Criminal Justice and Public Order Act 1994.* Bristol: Jordans.

**Carty, P.** (1996). 'Sab Fab?' *Time Out.* 26-19 June 1996.

**Chatterton, M.** (1976). 'Police in social control', in King, J.F.S. (ed.), *Control without Custody?* Cambridge: Institute of Criminology, p104-22.

**Clements, L. and Low-Beer, R.** (1996). 'Traveller Law Review'. *Legal Action.* January 1996. p11-13.

**Collin, M.** (1997). *Altered State: the Story of Ecstasy and Acid House.* London: Serpent's Tail.

**Cragg, S. and Low-Beer, R.** (1995). 'In defence of common humanity''. *New Law Journal.* September 15 1995, p1342-1343.

**Department of the Environment.** (1994). *Gypsy Sites Policy and Unauthorised Camping. Circular 18/94.* London: HMSO.

**Geary, R. and O'Shea, C.** (1995). 'Defining the traveller: from legal theory to practical action'. *Journal of Social Welfare and Family Law*, 17(2), p167-78.

**Home Office.** (1994). *Criminal Justice and Public Order Act 1994. Circular 45/94.* London: HMSO.

**Home Office.** (1992). *Guidance on the Policing of Hunts. Circular 11/92.* London: HMSO.

**Liberty.** (1995a). *Defend Diversity Defend Dissent: What's Wrong with the Criminal Justice and Public Order Act 1994.* London: Liberty.

**Liberty.** (1995b). *Criminalising Diversity Criminalising Dissent: a Report on the Use of the Public Order Provisions of the Criminal Justice and Public Order Act 1994.* London: Liberty.

**Penal Affairs Consortium.** (1994). *Squatters, Travellers, Ravers, Protesters and the Criminal Law.* London: Penal Affairs Consortium.

**Reiner, R.** (1992). *The Politics of the Police.* London: Harvester Wheatsheaf.

**Thornton, P.** (1994). 'Forgive our trespassers'. *The Times.* 8 March 1994.

**Vidal, J.** (1996). 'The bypass of justice'. *The Guardian.* 9 April 1996.

# Publications

## List of research publications

The most recent research reports published are listed below. A **full** list of publications is available on request from the Research, Development and Statistics Directorate, Information and Publications Group.

## Home Office Research Studies (HORS)

180.  **Sentencing Practice: an examination of decisions in magistrates's courts and the Crown Court in the mid–1990's.** Claire Flood-Page and Alan Mackie. 1998

181.  **Coroner service survey.** Roger Tarling. 1998.

182.  **The prevention of plastic and cheque fraud revisited.** Michael Levi and Jim Handley. 1998.

183.  **Drugs and crime: the results of research on drug testing and interviewing arrestees**. Trevor Bennett. 1998.

184.  **Remand decisions and offending on bail: evaluation of the Bail Process Project.** Patricia M Morgan and Paul F Henderson. 1998.

185.  **Entry into the criminal justice system: a survey of police arrests and their outcomes.** Coretta Phillips and David Brown with the assistance of Zoë James and Paul Goodrich. 1998

186.  **The restricted hospital order: from court to the community.** Robert Street. 1998

187.  **Reducing Offending: An assessment of research evidence on ways of dealing with offending behaviour.** Edited by Peter Goldblatt and Chris Lewis. 1998.

188.  **Lay visiting to police stations.** Mollie Weatheritt and Carole Vieira. 1998

189.  **Mandatory drug testing in prisons: The relationship between MDT and the level and nature of drug misuse.** Kimmett Edgar and Ian O'Donnell. 1998

## Research Findings

59. **Ethnicity and contacts with the police: latest findings from the British Crime Survey.** Tom Bucke. 1997.

60. **Policing and the public: findings from the 1996 British Crime Survey.** Catriona Mirrlees-Black and Tracy Budd. 1997.

61. **Changing offenders' attitudes and behaviour: what works?** Julie Vennard, Carol Hedderman and Darren Sugg. 1997.

62. **Suspects in police custody and the revised PACE codes of practice.** Tom Bucke and David Brown. 1997.

63. **Neighbourhood watch co-ordinators.** Elizabeth Turner and Banos Alexandrou. 1997.

64. **Attitudes to punishment: findings from the 1996 British Crime Survey.** Michael Hough and Julian Roberts. 1998.

65. **The effects of video violence on young offenders.** Kevin Browne and Amanda Pennell. 1998.

66. **Electronic monitoring of curfew orders: the second year of the trials.** Ed Mortimer and Chris May. 1998.

67. **Public perceptions of drug-related crime in 1997.** Nigel Charles. 1998.

68. **Witness care in magistrates' courts and the youth court.** Joyce Plotnikoff and Richard Woolfson. 1998.

69. **Handling stolen goods and theft: a market reduction approach.** Mike Sutton. 1998.

70. **Drug testing arrestees.** Trevor Bennett. 1998.

71. **Prevention of plastic card fraud.** Michael Levi and Jim Handley. 1998.

72. **Offending on bail and police use of conditional bail.** David Brown. 1998.

73. **Voluntary after-care.** Mike Maguire, Peter Raynor, Maurice Vanstone and Jocelyn Kynch. 1998.

74. **Fast-tracking of persistent young offenders.** John Graham. 1998.

75. **Mandatory drug testing in prisons – an evaluation.** Kimmett Edgar and Ian O'Donnell. 1998.

76. **The prison population in 1997: a statistical review.** Philip White. 1998.

77. **Rural areas and crime: findings from the British crime survey.** Catriona Mirrlees-Black. 1998.

78. **A review of classification systems for sex offenders.** Dawn Fisher and George Mair. 1998.

79. **An evaluation of the prison sex offender treatment programme.** Anthony Beech et al. 1998.

80. **Age limits for babies in prison: some lessons from abroad.** Diane Caddle. 1998.

81. **Motor projects in England & Wales: an evaluation.** Darren Sugg. 1998

82. **HIV/Aids risk behaviour among adult male prisoners.** John Strange et al. 1998.

83. **Concern about crime: findings from the 1998 British Crime Survey.** Catriona Mirrlees-Black and Jonathan Allen. 1998.

## Occasional Papers

**Evaluation of a Home Office initiative to help offenders into employment.** Ken Roberts, Alana Barton, Julian Buchanan and Barry Goldson. 1997.

**The impact of the national lottery on the horse-race betting levy.** Simon Field and James Dunmore. 1997.

**The cost of fires. A review of the information available.** Donald Roy. 1997.

**Monitoring and evaluation of WOLDS remand prison and comparisons with public-sector prisons, in particular HMP Woodhill.** A Keith Bottomley, Adrian James, Emma Clare and Alison Liebling. 1997.

## Requests for Publications

*Home Office Research Studies, Research Findings* and *Occasional Papers* can be requested from:

Research, Development and Statistics Directorate
Information and Publications Group
Room 201, Home Office
50 Queen Anne's Gate
London SW1H 9AT
Telephone: 0171-273 2084
Fascimile: 0171-222 0211
Internet: http://www.homeoffice.gov.uk/rds/index.htm
E-mail: rds.ho@gtnet.gov.uk